Ex-Inmate in Exile

The Autobiography of Philip A. Kumin

*BEST WISHES, ALWAYS,
TO STEVE AMRHEIN.*

Phil Kumin
6/28/93

American Literary Press
Owings Mills, Maryland

Ex-Inmate in Exile

Copyright © 1992 Philip A. Kumin

All rights reserved under International and Pan-American copyright conventions. No part of this book may be reproduced, stored in a retrieval system or transmitted in any form, electronic, mechanical, or other means, now known or hereafter invented, without written permission of the author. Address all inquiries to the author.

Library of Congress
Cataloging in Publication Data
ISBN 1-56167-106-1

Printed by

American Literary Press
11419 Cronridge Drive #10
Owings Mills, Maryland 21117

Manufactured in the United States of America

Back cover photo courtesy of
Craig Terkowitz and the *Baltimore Jewish Times*.

Acknowledgements

Gratitude is extended to John K. McComb for his critiquing of my manuscript. Gratitude is also extended to Janet Kozlay, of the Baltimore Writers' Alliance, for her critiquing of such as well. Lastly, my thanks to Michael W. Skojec, Esquire, for his review of the manuscript for legal appropriateness.

When I think of the inspiration John Lennon, Paul McCartney, George Harrison, and Ringo Starr have always been to me, I think most immediately, of the beautiful photograph of the four of them used on their *Beatles VI* album cover. As you can see, they're always, always smiling and giving me a reason to laugh myself, no matter what. God Bless You, all four of you, forever. And, thanks.

And what words can I use to thank Jim Morrison, Robbie Krieger, Ray Manzarek, and John Densmore? Could I possibly have made it without the promise your dark and beautiful poetry has always held for me? Uh-uh.

I always had Jim's ironic spirit near me in times of crisis. Whenever I thought I couldn't see any alternative to demise, Jim would suddenly turn his face upwards at me, give me one of his mischievous and bizarre smiles, and tell me, "Don't give up, there's still something to live for: our poetry."

And Jim has always been right.

-- Philip Andre Kumin

Chapter One

My mother once told me I was born around 3:00 p.m. on the date of my birth, February 25, 1953. I recall she said I was born at the "old" Sinai Hospital, then located in East Baltimore.

My father, Howard J. Kumin, was then a labor statistician for the United Nations, assigned to assess and implement labor programs throughout Latin America. I was the youngest of three, my brother Gerson having been born in 1941, and my sister Susie in 1945.

My earliest recollections are of a house that we lived in and a car that we owned in Bogota, Colombia. I was perhaps two years old when we arrived in Colombia for a 14-month stay, on one of my father's regional assignments. I have memories of touring the salt mines of Cali, and of the open-air meat market at a place called "Chia." I have memories of traveling through the lush mountains by train. I remember bending over to look at the red-hot boiler underneath the steam engine at one point at which we had stopped. I remember being frightened by the hissing of steam.

Perhaps one of my most vivid memories from that time was of the rural Latin American airport from which we departed the day of our return to the United States. Immediately beyond a small wooden building which served as a terminal lay the airport's lone dirt runway. However, off to the right of this same building was an open storage area where several rows of Lockheed Constellations were tethered to the ground. Most of these belonged to the

Colombian airline, Avianca. We had time to kill before the departure of our flight, and so Susie walked me around this deserted, quiet, gravel apron. It was there, that day, that I learned the meanings of the words "fuselage" and "aileron," and there that I began a long love affair with airplanes.

We returned in the late 1950s to the same northwestern part of Baltimore City where my mother, father and sister had been living when I was born. At that point, this neighborhood was still predominantly white and Jewish, though already in the beginning stages of transition from white to black.

Susie and I were both born in Baltimore at Sinai Hospital. However, at the time that Gerson was born, my parents were living in the Washington metropolitan area, and thus he was born in a Washington, D.C., hospital. Gerson was also the only one of the three of us who was delivered by natural childbirth. Unfortunately, the attending obstetrician used a pair of forceps on my brother's head in an effort to pry him loose from my mother's birth canal, causing him lasting brain damage. To this day, Gerson suffers from a seizure disorder.

Partially because of his misunderstood seizure disorder, and partially because of ill effects that my father had had on my brother's psychological development, it was recommended that Gerson be sent to an experimental extension of the University of Chicago, known as the Orthogenic School, run by the late psychiatrist Dr. Bruno Bettelheim. It was here that he resided at the time of my birth, although he returned shortly thereafter to accompany us to Bogota. When we returned to Baltimore after that, my mother enrolled me in a nearby nursery school,

Susie entered the sixth grade, and Gerson began public high school. My father continued to work and travel overseas.

Though my maternal grandfather (whom I never knew, but have always wished I had) was a native Baltimorean, my mother's mother was born and raised in London, England. It was here as well that my mother, Hazel Edna Goldman, the first of four girls, was born, though my grandparents returned to Baltimore soon thereafter. Mother was born in 1913, and it wasn't long before the rest of the Lyon family, including my great Aunt Miriam, followed my grandmother, Lillian, to America.

My paternal grandparents, Sadie and Max Kumin, were born and raised in the Baltic country of Latvia, later annexed by the Soviet Union. My father, the first of three boys, was born in Brockton, Massachusetts, in 1907, after my grandparents had emigrated to the U.S. Though Susie, Gerson and I were always raised much more closely to our mother's side of the family than our father's, we nonetheless visited our aunts, uncles and cousins in New England.

My recollection of my father's father is that he was the complete personal opposite of his wife. Though extremely hard of hearing, whenever one was able to communicate with him, one discovered what a very warm, jovial, affable person he was. By contrast, my vague memory of my grandmother is that she was always angry, chiding, castigating of other people, and never satisfied with anyone else's performance, just as my own father has never been.

Sadly, my father has always taken after his mother. His frustration with the realities of life, for whatever existential reasons, has never permitted him to carry on a normal social discourse with others. He has remained a social anarchist.

Chapter Two

One other member of our family was our maid, Ruth, a large black woman.

A toy which had been in our family for many years prior to my time was a life-sized baby doll. This doll had a device implanted in it which would emit a crying sound whenever the doll was turned over. One day, in proximity to the date my mother was due to deliver me, Susie and Gerson played a trick on Ruth. They tucked this doll in under the covers in a crib my mother had set up in anticipation of my arrival.

Ruth came rushing into work one morning, glanced at the crib without looking very closely at what was in it, and exclaimed out loud, "Oh, my Lord! He's been born already!"

Although Ruth despised my father (and he her), she loved us dearly and loved my mother as much as we did. One day when my mother and father were in the midst of a horrendous fight, she threatened my father that if he so much as raised his fist at my mother one more time, she would knock him flat.

Even though Ruth had blood relatives of her own in the Baltimore area, to her we were her family. She was overjoyed when my mother accepted an invitation from her, on behalf of all of us, to have dinner with her at her home. I was thrilled when my mother gave Ruth permission to take me home for a weekend.

Sometimes in life, we all acquire memories of events we would just as soon prefer to forget. I remember, unfortunately, at age six, falling into the company of several semi-delinquent kids who lived down the street from us. One afternoon, after playing with these kids for a while, I came home looking for a fight. Ruth was in the kitchen attending to matters there. Although I do not recall at this point what it was she said to me, I do remember telling her to "shut her shit black mouth up!"

Ruth whirled and bore down on me. When she reached me, she grabbed my arm and shook me. Never will I forget the look of hurt and anger that filled her face. Nor will I forget the way her jaw trembled. She screamed at me, "Don't you ever talk to me that way!" She also swore she was going to tell my father about this when he arrived home. (He happened to be in town at the time.) Sure enough, she did, and when I realized she was going to go through with this, I began to cry in front of my father. Before she had even finished telling him what had happened, he had put two and two together and had figured out what had gone on. To his credit this time, for taking Ruth's side of things, he delivered a stern warning to me not to ever do this kind of thing again. I believe I got out of a beating that night, but I had been sufficiently shaken up.

Chapter Three

My father, indeed, was both the direct and indirect instigator of the domestic violence that occurred in my family. One night, my father began picking and picking and picking away at my brother until finally Gerson lashed out at him, and a bloody, protracted fight ensued. My brother and father rolled on the floor, biting, scratching, punching, and cursing at each other. This seemed to go on endlessly, and when my mother could not break it up, she finally screamed, grabbed me by the hand, and walked out of the house with me in tow, to wait outside until it was all over. We returned a while later, by which time, fortunately, the fight was over. My brother and father sat, literally, at opposite ends of the room, licking their wounds and glaring at each other.

A terrible silence filled the air. I do not recall where my sister was that night.

One other night, when I was perhaps five or six, I was lying awake after my mother had put me to bed. I was listening to the rising tide of a loud argument between my mother and my brother just outside my room. All of a sudden my mother screamed in pain and began to cry. My brother had punched her in the stomach and broken one of her ribs.

There was another time, several years later, when my mother was fixing dinner, and my brother and I were both watching television. My mother announced dinner was ready, and at that point, Gerson snapped the TV off in his most favorite dictatorial way. He was well aware I wanted to see the end of the cartoon we were watching, but he switched off the TV anyway. I protested, and my mother reprimanded my brother for being unnecessarily cruel to me. At that point, Gerson picked me up and threw me against a table leg. I split my head open, requiring numerous stitches to close the wound, on an emergency basis.

In each of these cases, I do not recall where Susie was, but I do know where my father always was. Overseas. He was home periodically between assignments. But the problem was that when he was home, life was even more hellish than it was, at times, when he was gone.

Chapter Four

When my mother, sister, brother and I had returned to Baltimore from Colombia, my father had not come back with us. Instead, he had embarked on a five-year tour of duty to India, Nepal and Pakistan, directly from Bogota. Though Susie and Gerson had opportunities to travel with him for periods of time in the Far East, I was too young to do so, and so my mother and I remained in Baltimore.

Early one evening, I came indoors from playing with my friends to see if dinner was ready yet. I noticed a strange man with a mustache sitting in the living room as I passed through on my way back to the kitchen where my mother was fixing dinner. I noticed him follow me with his eyes as I paraded by, a slight smile of amusement on his face as he watched me. When I found my mom, I whispered to her, "Who's that man out front?"

She replied, "That's your father."

I was dumbstruck. My *what*?! Consciously, I was unaware it took two to make a baby, and that, therefore, my mother was not all that existed in the universe. And yet, when I asked him if he really was my daddy, and he said, "Yes," I instinctively became very excited. Suddenly I had a completely unexpected feeling of wholeness.

There were at least two occasions when my mother left my father after having had a bitter argument with him. Sadly, she always came back the next day, after spending the night in a hotel somewhere. She would always take me with her, though she would leave Susie and Gerson with him.

On at least one occasion I can remember, my father struck my mother in full view of the three of us. Partially out of shock, and partially out of a determination to shield us from trauma, she made light of it several hours later.

One final compounding factor in my early childhood life was my mother's poor physical health. Along with mental illness, diabetes was something which ran hereditarily in her side of our family. My mother was inflicted with a substantial case of it, as was a first cousin of mine. Thus, my mother suffered all the accompanying physical ailments, among them, poor circulation, an eventual heart condition, and premature aging in general. Susie once remarked, after my mother's death, that my mother's health had begun a gradual decline soon after I was born. My mother spent a substantial portion of my early life in the hospital. When Mother was away, Susie would frequently assume the household duties of cooking, cleaning, and seeing to it that I was in bed each night, in addition to keeping up with her own schoolwork.

We all have memories of particularly golden moments in our lives, which we end up treasuring to such a degree that they sometimes take on the quality of the stuff that dreams are made of. One night during a period of time when Mom was in the hospital, Susie, as usual, fixed dinner for me. She then put me to bed and read me what was one of the most phantasmagoric bedtime stories I had ever been captivated by at that age. Then she kissed me goodnight and left the room.

If there is any kind of special relationship that exists between a little Jewish boy and his Big Sister, I was bonded to Susie in that way that night.

Chapter Five

I was, of course, unaware of the submerged cauldron of troublesome factors brewing in my life at this time, and so I felt happy. Against all odds, my mother succeeded in providing us with a secure home life, when she was well enough to do so.

Upon completion of my father's five-year assignment in the Far East, he returned home for an interlude before being sent to West Africa for the next several years. In 1962, he was asked to write one type or another of handbook on labor matters in Switzerland. This gave us the opportunity to go abroad ourselves and to spend the summer traveling through Europe before meeting him in Geneva. By the end of that year, however, he had once again been sent to Latin America.

On one of my father's visits home from this most recent Latin American assignment, he told us that for the foreseeable future he would be working in numerous countries throughout Central and South America once again. He and my mother began discussing the fact that our relocating down there would give us an opportunity to see him more often than if we remained in the U.S. They began making plans for us to do so.

In the fall of 1963, my parents chose Chile as the country in which we would settle. One day, however, in the midst of our preparations to move, Mom received a long-distance phone call from her next youngest sister, Sylvia. Sylvia and her husband Normand had a daughter, my cousin Anita, who was also diagnosed with diabetes.

Sylvia told Mom about a research center in Boston, known as the Joslin Clinic, that specialized in the treatment of diabetes where Anita had been successfully treated. Sylvia implored my mother to check into this clinic herself, and my mother thought well of the idea. By October, we were ready to vacate our rented house in Baltimore and begin the journey that would end in Santiago, the capital of Chile. Susie, by this time, had graduated from high school and had begun her freshman year at Antioch College in Ohio. Upon our departure from Baltimore, however, both my mother and my brother went to the Joslin Clinic so Mom could be treated and Gerson could receive instruction in how to care properly for her afterwards.

Chapter Six

Sylvia and Normand were fond of telling the story of how a maid of theirs could not pronounce my Uncle Normand's Hebrew name "Tulke" correctly. She called him "Tookie" instead, and the name stuck.

Later on in my life, I was to learn my father had always thought Tookie to be an arrogant blowhard whom he didn't care for. Tookie had a Jewish machismo way of insisting everyone adhere to the same straight-arrow lifestyle that he did, a holdover from his Army days. Back then, however, he also had a very good sense of humor as well, and as children, we loved him.

While Mother and Gerson were at the Joslin Clinic attending to matters there, Sylvia and Tookie took care of me. I spent this period of time with them at their house in Virginia.

In his own way, Uncle Tookie did closely fit the portrait of the warm, benevolent American father. In his own way, he was always a very moral, dignified man as well, in precisely all the same ways my own father has never been. In fact, memories of my Uncle Tookie as he was when I was a child have many times served as inspirations to me. I remember well one day when Tookie and I went over to a field across from their house to fly a gas model airplane. I remember how morally furious both Sylvia and Tookie became when they learned a friend of their son David had swindled me out of some money.

Chapter Seven

As may already be known, the United Nations is composed of numerous specialized agencies which deal with specific kinds of universal issues. These include, among others, the Food and Agriculture Organization, the World Health Organization, the World Bank, and the United Nations' International Children's Emergency Fund, more commonly known as U.N.I.C.E.F. By 1963, my father had been transferred into the International Labor Organization from his previous post within the U.N.-at-large.

We arrived in Santiago in December of 1963, spending Christmas and New Year's in a rented apartment my father's office had procured for us in anticipation of our arrival. We remained in this temporary housing through the middle of February 1964. During this time, we awaited delivery of our 1963 Chevrolet Impala, which my father had purchased in the U.S. for $3000, but which he had had shipped down to us. When our car arrived, we were then able to make daily excursions throughout the city of Santiago looking for more permanent housing. Santiago, at the time, had a population of approximately 2 million people.

At length, we located and secured housing suitable to our needs. By then, we had also received word that our household belongings, which my parents likewise had shipped down, had arrived at the Pacific port of Valparaiso.

Valparaiso sits immediately next to a resort area known as "Con-Con," in the middle segment of the long

EX-INMATE IN EXILE

Chilean coast. My parents decided we should make a festive occasion out of our journey to the Pacific, to make arrangements for our belongings to be transported back to Santiago. Mom and Dad rented rooms for all of us at a nearby tourist hotel once we arrived, and over the next several days, we toured the sights of this local area.

South of the Equator, the seasons are reversed from what they are in the United States, which means that by February or March of each year, the Autumn season is approaching. Nevertheless, the beaches for which Con-Con is known were packed.

Never having seen any part of the Pacific Ocean before, I was impressed with the relative cleanliness of the water in comparison to that of the Atlantic. Neither had I seen surf to the extent that one could go surfing in the water, as is the case along the west coasts of all of the Americas. I lacked a board, but this was no stop to me. I waded out to the point at which the water was up to my chest, waited for a swell to come, and then jumped in front of it, allowing it to catch me as it swept by. I pretended I was Superman as I lay with my arms outstretched in front of me, my body perpetually beneath the crest of the wave. I was aloft, though by way of water rather than by air. As we neared the beach, I began to scrape the bottom. I was unceremoniously deposited on the beach, on my belly, arms still outstretched, with a bathing suit full of sand.

My recollection of the rest of this vacation is of evenings spent eating "corvina" in open-air restaurants around Con-Con. Corvina is the name for a particularly scrumptious kind of fish which swims in the South Pacific. Sadly, I do not know the English translation of this name, or whether this fish may be available in markets on the

East Coast of the United States. The only thing that mars these pleasant memories is the memory of my mother and father's almost constant bickering.

My mother and father made arrangements for our belongings to be transported back to Santiago aboard a flatbed tractor-trailer truck. Our possessions had been shipped in huge wooden crates known as "lift-vans." These were loaded onto the truck which then followed us back across the mountains to our new home. My recollection is that Santiago and Valparaiso/Con-Con were an approximate 90-minute drive apart.

The next several weeks were spent uncrating and unpacking. My father constructed a makeshift portico out of an entire wooden side of one of the crates. He, Gerson, and I then hoisted this to the top of a garden wall which surrounded our backyard and mounted it in place. Accordingly, my dad then slung his most treasured possession under the shade of this new portico. As he lay in his hammock, we knew that Paradise had been achieved.

Mom and Dad had rented Chile's version of a row-house for us, thinking such an accommodation would be warmer in winter than any free-standing house. At this time, only the most majestic of houses in Santiago had oil or steam-driven central heating systems. If a family was lucky, it may have been able to live in a house which had a semi-centralized heating system that burned paraffin oil. But most houses were equipped only with fireplaces, thereby necessitating the purchase of additional, individual paraffin stoves. Cooking stoves ran on propane gas, piped in from containers kept outside while in use. Replenished bottles of gas were available by delivery. Chopped firewood was plentiful and cheap, and accordingly, air pollution was terrible in winter.

We happened to have our own telephone; however, this did us little good. At the time, Santiago was not sufficiently wired for every house to have a telephone. Though telephone service was not nonexistent, it was rare. Even when one was able to obtain phone service, a party line was all that was available.

In America, live-in servants are exclusively aristocratic accoutrements. Throughout Latin America, however, the retention of paid servants is entirely middle-class in nature. Servants' quarters are always located immediately off the kitchen area in any conventional house. Hired servants, at the time almost always women, doubled as nannies for the care of small children.

My father once told us while we were still in Baltimore that American-made cars were seen about as frequently in Chile as Cadillacs were in the U.S. at the time. In fact, American cars were a sought-after commodity in Chile back then. My father had purchased our new 1963 Chevy Impala for $3000 in the U.S., yet 18 months later, he was able to sell it in Santiago for the equivalent of $10,000 American dollars.

The vast majority of motor vehicles in Santiago, were small European-made automobiles. Hundreds of motorcycles, motorbikes, and motor scooters all contributed further to an already serious pollution problem.

Public transit in this South American capital consisted of three different kinds of bus systems, along with electrically-operated trolley buses.

Colorfully marked school buses, known as "micros" (pronounced "meek-ros"), functioned as the mainstay of the transit system. These differed from American school buses in that they had rear exit doors as well as front entrance doors. Upon boarding these buses, one would place one's fare in a rudimentary farebox and receive a small, preprinted ticket as a receipt, about the size of a large stamp. Continuous transfers were not issued between vehicles. If one needed to take more than one bus in order to reach one's destination, one was expected to pay anew each time one boarded another vehicle. Fares, however, were a pittance.

During rush hours, not only would there be passengers standing in the aisles of these buses once the seats were filled, but people would hang out the front and back doors as well. Handle grips were mounted on the outside of the buses near the doors expressly for this purpose. Frequently, people would crawl onto the roofs and hoods of these buses also, though taking care not to obstruct the drivers' view. These passengers would simply hold on for dear life as the vehicles sped away.

One afternoon, I was returning from school with a tremendous armload of books not held together by any strap. Foolishly, I boarded a very crowded micro and gripped the handle bar just beneath the rear-view mirror mount with one free hand. Fortunately for me, there was still someone else doing the same thing behind me, astoundingly enough. (They really packed these buses.)

Ever so slowly, we pulled away from the curb. Just as we had gathered momentum, the top-most book under my arm began to slip. (A Bible, no kidding. Religious education was compulsory in the school I was attending.) The Bible fell, and the man holding on behind me graciously caught it between his feet for me. Like a real ass, I tried to retrieve my Bible and lost my balance in the process. (Something from within the pages of this holy book must have enabled me to remember not to let go of the handle grip.) As the bus raced along, I swung out freely, remaining books under my arm and all. A huge woman in the front seat screamed, stood up, grabbed me, and literally hauled me back into the doorway of the bus. It was only at this point that the driver, hitherto oblivious to what was going on, realized something was wrong and began to apply the brakes.

Dear Readers, I promise you this story is the Gospel truth. (Perhaps there should be a pun here!)

A second kind of transit bus that operated in Santiago was a smaller, speedier kind of Mercedes-Benz microbus, known in Spanish as a "liebre" ("hare" in English). These would zip around the city in augmentation of the micros' routes, and were slightly more expensive in fare.

The third type of bus used was a large diesel-driven one, all of which were painted a standardized green and white, as were the electric trolley buses. The diesel buses, as well as the trolley buses, were owned and operated by the state, whereas the micros and liebres were privately owned and operated.

The elementary and secondary school systems in Santiago were predominantly private. Such as was the case in the retention of servants, sending one's children to one of the almost myriad of private schools in the city was an entirely middle-class custom. There was a public school system in Santiago, but this was attended only by the children of the poor. Chilean society did appear to have been class distinctive at the time. Regrettably, I have no information concerning the quality of education rendered in the public school system there, either at that time or the present.

I attended a British school known as "The Grange." This was an Old-Worldian all-boys school which was composed of both boarding and day students, and where corporal punishment was meted out. Here, fully 40% of the students were native Chileans, 30% were Americans, 20% were British, and 10% were of other nationalities. The faculty and administrators of the school were predominantly British, and the school used a British system of advancement known as "the Common Entrances." Artful Dodgers that we were, we studied and recreationalized in the midst of a world of Charles Dickens'.

Just as all my peers do, when I think of the year 1964, more than anything else I think of four fellows who entered my life, and upon eventually leaving it, left it in such a way that the world would never seem the same for me again. Beatlemania may have been even more intense in South America than in North America, particularly at the Grange School. Back then, anything whatsoever that was British was absolute gold.

To my knowledge, the Beatles never toured Latin America. One day, however, a friend of mine from school told me about some rave movie called *A Hard Day's Night* which was playing at a theater in downtown Santiago. Fascinated by the oxymoron, and sensing, somehow, I was on the brink of some major life-change, I accepted his invitation to go see it. When we arrived at the theater, we found a line of people waiting to get in stretching several blocks back. We worked our way through the line, stayed long enough to see the continuously playing movie twice, were witnessed, baptized, and we left so others could get in. Outside, street vendors made a killing selling baseball cards with photographs of John, Paul, George and Ringo on them, along with other memorabilia. The bus we caught home was nearly full of people who had just exited from seeing *A Hard Day's Night*, as had we. Choruses of Beatles' songs reverberated around the bus all the way through the city. My friend, Dennis, and I had an advantage, however. We could sing in English.

Chile was the first part of the world I had been in where earthquakes were a fact of life. The same fault line which begins in Alaska and runs south through California continues on down the west coasts of all three Americas. I once overheard someone saying the earthquakes occurring in Chile were of a more volcanic nature than of being due to the shifting of plates within the earth. In Santiago, most tremors occurred in the evening and were preceded by three or four seconds of a low rumbling sound coming from deep within the earth before the actual quaking would begin. I was mortally terrified by each of these events. I would jump up and down in fear, knowing that for those brief seconds during which time my feet were not on the ground I would not have to feel that awful trembling through the floor.

One day, a friend of mine and his mother asked me if I would like to join them on a three-week trip to the south of Chile. Michael's father worked for a company which owned one of the world's largest farms, located some sixty miles from the southern city of Osorno. The primary product marketed by this farm was wood.

My mother and father thought this would be an excellent educational opportunity for me, and so they gave their consent for me to accompany Michael, his mother, and his younger brother, Carlos, on this voyage.

Upon our arrival in Osorno by air, an official from the farm met us and drove us to a nearby boat landing. We boarded one of a fleet of steamboats used for transporting lumber up and down the river which spanned the length of the distance between the farm and Osorno. This was a river which ultimately emptied out into the Pacific.

We cruised for three or four hours, during which time darkness fell. As there was no electricity in this region, or on the farm, we arrived at our destination in complete darkness.

Over the next several weeks, Michael and I rode on horseback for miles and miles on end each day before returning. Though motor vehicles were owned by the farm, horses were the principle means of getting around. Accordingly, a blacksmith was kept busy pounding out red-hot horseshoes day in and day out.

Though it was warm while we were there, during winter it is very cold in that region, and each year much snow falls. The rooms in the farmhouse where we stayed were heated only by pot-bellied stoves. Likewise, the kitchen stove burned wood. Candles lit the rooms at night.

Next to our farmhouse was a curing house where sides of beef and poultry were hung. At one point, Michael's mother asked for beef for dinner, and a steer was butchered accordingly. One other day, I walked outside to find one of the ranch hands draining the blood out of a decapitated turkey, holding it upside down in order to do so. The headless bird would occasionally flap its wings. While we were there, the news that the United States had committed troops to Vietnam reached us.

By the time it was time for us to return home, I was ready to leave. The farm was very isolated, and I had become homesick. Years later, when reading John Steinbeck's *East of Eden*, I envisioned this farm as the setting for the story.

During the time we lived in Chile, we received word that my mother's aunt, Miriam Lyon, had passed away in Spring Grove State Hospital located in Catonsville, Maryland. Many years later, Susie was to tell me that Aunt Miriam had had a diagnosis of manic depression. Sylvia, however, was to tell me Aunt Miriam had had a diagnosis of "dementia praecox," an old name for schizophrenia. What is most likely, unfortunately, is that they really didn't know what was wrong with Aunt Miriam. Back in those days, doctors were only slightly less able to make accurate diagnoses than they remain today.

Many a Saturday afternoon Mother would pack the three of us and herself into the Volkswagen, and we would be off to southwestern Baltimore County. I remember well ascending to the top of the Catonsville exit ramp off Baltimore's Beltway, coming to rest at Frederick Road. My mother would curse the perennial potholes which ran the length of Wade Avenue leading to "The Grove," as it is fondly known today.

We would come to visit Aunt Miriam and take her for a ride in the countryside. We would stop somewhere for an ice cream cone or two before "escorting" her back to the hospital. I remember how, upon arrival back at Spring Grove, Mom would slowly and sadly walk Aunt Miriam back to the ward on which she lived. In those days, I had no idea why it always took Mom so long to return to the car after walking Aunt Miriam back to her hall. I didn't have any idea that one day when I was older I was going to find out.

Aunt Miriam entered Spring Grove while in her 20s, soon after her arrival in America from England. She died there at either age 79 or 80. She suffered from diabetes as well.

Chapter Eight

Soon after we had settled into our new house in Santiago, Mom suffered a heart attack. The night she became ill, she sent Gerson to call for an ambulance on a neighbor's telephone, as we had none of our own.

Mom was later to say she believed the shock of John F. Kennedy's assassination, coupled with the stress of moving, had brought on her heart condition. Under any circumstances, she suffered a second heart attack while there, as well as a bout with pneumonia. By May of 1965, it was necessary for her to return to the U.S. under emergency circumstances. She flew to Houston, Texas, in order to undergo surgery by Dr. Michael DeBakey. Prior to her death three years later, she was operated on at least one other time by Dr. DeBakey, as well as once by his assistant, Dr. Denton Cooley.

Susie had flown down for a second time, this time to help us pack up and return to the States. In July, we said farewell to life in South America for the second time and came home.

It was acknowledged that Mom was no longer going to be able to drive an automobile, and so a decision was made that upon our return to the States we should settle in the Northern Virginia area rather than in Baltimore again. Mom knew she would feel more comfortable being close to Sylvia and Tookie, on whom she could depend for transportation and moral support. We rented a modern, air-conditioned, three-bedroom apartment that was otherwise in a white, hillbilly slum area of Alexandria.

Mom then enrolled me in the sixth grade in a nearby elementary school. My parents decided they wanted me to receive a Bar Mitzvah, and as I was fast approaching my thirteenth birthday, I was enrolled in religious school as well at Temple Beth-El in Alexandria. I was Bar Mitzvahed there on March 19, 1966.

I was growing up into my adolescence, and with this was developing a need to distance myself from my mother, whom I had been entirely too emotionally dependent upon as a small child. I became terribly uncomfortable around her and fought bitterly with her as a result. My mother, however, was wise and recognized what I was experiencing. She contacted a private counseling agency in nearby Arlington and arranged for me to have an interview with one of their psychologists as a prelude to my participating in a group therapy program there. Not at all surprisingly, my recollection of this psychologist is that he was highly cold and aloof.

This was my first contact ever with the mental health system, and I was terrified. My mother, again wisely, wrote down my fears for me one evening as she was saying goodnight to me. The next day, I took them to the psychologist, whose replies, sadly, I do not now recall. I do not remember all the worries I had, but I do remember my chief two were, "What was being crazy like?" and "Was I going to get that way?!"

I was placed in a therapy group composed of three or four other boys my age, all of whom were rough-and-tumble, smart-allecky, and rowdy as hell. The group was facilitated by another aloof and bored psychiatrist. My crowning glory, however, was in attempting to seriously discuss a problem I had in the midst of this otherwise cacophony. At this, our bored psychiatrist came suddenly to life and encouraged me to go on. This made me feel good.

My mother realized I was reluctant to go, and when I began missing group meetings, she decided to look for a different program for me elsewhere in the area. She contacted the Alexandria Community Mental Health Center, and I began attending meetings there. This group was led by a black man named Bill Taylor who introduced himself as a "psychiatric social worker." Considering I had no idea whatsoever what a "psychiatric social worker" was at the time, it is ironic I remembered his title for so many years afterwards.

I did, indeed, gain much from these sessions, and after a while I began looking forward to them each week, never missing a-one. Mr. Taylor was a cool, hip guy, a creative facilitator and an excellent role model. Periodically, he would introduce other social work students into our meetings who actively participated in fulfillment of their internships. The members of the group served as role models to each other as well.

Chapter Nine

Once while a day student at the Grange School in Santiago, I commented to my parents that I wondered what it would be like to attend boarding school. My mother and father had never forgotten this remark, and as my mother's physical health continued to deteriorate, my idea was resurrected. My mother approached the Alexandria Community Mental Health Center for referrals, and of those given us by them, we narrowed our choice down to a school located in Berkshire County, Massachusetts. We were told that Dr. Hans K. Maeder, the director of the Stockbridge School, would be recruiting for students in the Washington area in April of that year. Soon after having had an interview with him, we received word I had been accepted for admission. Accordingly, in September of 1967, I got my first taste of life away from home.
 When I arrived at the Stockbridge School, I was suddenly thrust into the midst of a peer social environment I had never been exposed to before. Fourteen years old at the time, I was still dressing in the preppy, buttoned-down-collar style of dress favored by Southern men and boys in states like Virginia back in the 1960s. When I arrived in Stockbridge, I encountered 139 tough students, predominantly from the New York metropolitan area, who wore way-out outfits and listened to bizarre music by artists with such names as "The Jimi Hendrix Experience," "Cream," "The Doors," "The Jefferson Airplane," and "Country Joe and the Fish." Most of these kids also came

from rich families, which meant they had the money to buy something else I had never encountered before either: drugs.

The Berkshires are beautiful, and the memories of gazing out of my open dormitory window at the surrounding forested hills in autumn are what have sustained me ever since. I would sit and gaze through the window on a crisp afternoon sometime in October of 1967. The rhapsody of "The Masked Marauder" would tumble in from the open window of one of the other students' rooms on the floor above me. On a weekend afternoon, Randy Connell, his roommate Dave Pedroni, Mike Martin, and I would hike and climb for two hours to the summit of one of the Berkshire hills immediately behind the school's campus, returning in time for dinner in the school's dining hall. When I reflect back on those golden afternoons now, I remember the sunlight filtering through the trees as we moved on through the forest. As we left the dormitory further and further behind us, the strains of, perhaps, "You're Lost, Little Girl" would grow faint and more and more distant as we jaunted farther and farther along.

Hans Maeder always told us we were students in Stockbridge in order to be educated for democracy. The philosophers Bertrand Russell and Albert Schweitzer were idols of his, and he quoted liberally from them. In addition to regularly scheduled classes, sports and extracurricular activities, weekly school meetings were held in the lounge area of one of the larger dormitories. Modeled after New England Town Meetings, Hans would always remind us, nonetheless, that he retained the final veto power over any collective decisions made he did not feel would be in the school's best interest. However, with this exception, these two-hour meetings would be true exercises in parliamentary procedure and participatory democracy. During our best meetings, we truly debated the fate of the world and what our position in that should be.

One decision made by the school as a whole in January of 1968 was for those students who so chose to be able to participate in demonstrations against the war in Vietnam. This was a decision which Hans condoned, and for the next several Saturdays, we bused to nearby Pittsfield for these marches, which grew larger each week. Later on that year, Lyndon Johnson announced he would not run for reelection. This then became my first taste of what we refer to today as "empowerment."

Chapter Ten

All during that spring, my mother was seriously ill, spending almost the entire season in one hospital or another. In April, I was notified I was going to be permitted to fly home for the weekend, as my mother, who had just endured an amputation, was near death. I did rush home, where I was joined by Gerson, Sylvia and Tookie, my mother's other two sisters Elyse and Helen Gene, Susie home from Antioch, and my father up from Ecuador. My mother was in the intensive care unit at Georgetown University Hospital where she was hooked up to a heart monitoring device. We were not permitted to visit with her for more than a moment, as she was very weak and only semiconscious. But by the end of that very tense weekend, we were able to gain hope from the fact her heart rhythm had improved, and so we felt more secure in returning to our respective corners of the earth.

The end of the school year came on June 9 that year. After getting a ride to the New York area with one of my friends and his uncle, I flew the rest of the way to Washington, D.C..

The following day, my first day home for the summer, Gerson and I went to visit Mom who, though improved, was still in the hospital. A friend of hers had come to pick us up and drove us to visit her. Mother was considerably more alert than she had been while in intensive care, but she seemed depressed and in poor spirits. While we were there, her doctor had a frank consultation with us. He told us, honestly, that with the numerous complications she had, if she went in one direction, she would survive. If she went in the other, she would not. I left the hospital that afternoon more depressed and upset than I had ever been before. Out of exhaustion, I fell asleep in the back seat of my mother's friend's car on the way home.

Back in March, during spring vacation when Susie was also home, she had announced she was getting married upon her graduation from Antioch that year. She told us her fiance was a black student from Central State University in Ohio, who likewise would be graduating from college that spring.

Ironically, the same evening Gerson and I returned home from having received the terrible news about Mom while visiting her was the same evening Gerson and I met our future relative for the first time. It was positively bizarre to be so upset about Mom on one hand and so excited about meeting our impending brother-in-law on the other.

Gerson and I were sitting at home in the depths of despair that evening when a friendly knock came at the door. I jumped up first and, peering through the peephole, I was surprised to see a very tall man smiling at me from behind Susie. I opened the door, and Susie introduced us to William Joseph Harris, who came to be known to us more simply as Billy Joe, or Billy. Billy turned out to be a very warm, jovial, well-educated person with an excellent sense of humor, who was also very gentle and kind. He was an instant smash with both Gerson and me.

Over the next week, the four of us spent our time sightseeing, shopping and getting to know each other. We visited Mother every day in the hospital.

Mother had most likely anticipated she wasn't going to live much longer, and she wanted to be certain I would be looked after when she had left us. Caring for me as she always had, she had made arrangements from her hospital bed for me to become a counselor-in-training at a summer camp in Western Maryland. Susie reassured Mom she would not permit me to depart for camp without seeing to it that I had all of the belongings I would need beforehand.

At the end of the week, Susie, Billy and I said goodbye to Mom and Gerson and prepared to leave for Billy's hometown of Yellow Springs, Ohio. Billy's parents had bought Susie and him their first automobile as a wedding-present-in-advance, and we prepared for the long ride in front of us. As there were still several weeks ahead before I was to begin camp, it was thought best that I go with Susie and Billy back to Ohio so I could see some place new and could meet Billy's family there.

We arrived at Susie's off-campus apartment in Yellow Springs after an exhausting 12-hour ride through Virginia, West Virginia, Pennsylvania and Ohio. I took up residence on Susie's couch.

My father, who had likewise graduated from Antioch many years earlier, said even back then the school had had a freaky, avant-garde reputation. In 1968, however, the college and the town were in the throes of flower power and related psychedelia. I was thrilled that Antioch's dormitories were open to visitors of the opposite sex and that, therefore, I could pass freely through the women's dorms, in spite of the fact I was male. Members of either sex were strictly forbidden from being in the dorms of the opposite one at the Stockbridge School because of our younger ages.

Over the next several days, I frequented Antioch's student library. I spent hours gazing out the window of the record listening room on the second floor of the building, glued to my headphones. I was lost in the rapture of "Disraeli Gears" as I stared out across the campus, bathed in summer sunlight.

On my third day there, I returned to Susie's house after having spent time in the library. I entered Susie's kitchen through the rear screen door and instantaneously knew something was terribly wrong. Hearing me come in, Susie came in to greet me from the next room. After one look at her face, I knew the unthinkable had happened. Her mouthing of the words, therefore, was merely after-the-fact. Mom had died.

I made it over to the kitchen table where I collapsed in a chair and cried without stopping for the next three hours.

One by one, Susie's neighbors filed in to comfort me and to comfort us. Plans were made for us to fly immediately to Baltimore, where we were met by old friends of our family with whom we stayed. My father flew up from Ecuador, and within a week my mother had been buried. This was the first funeral I had ever attended. Though we had an open-casket memorial service, I chose to remember my mother as she had been when I was a little boy.

One of my most bizarre memories was of my father's reaction to my mother's death. At one point, he kept saying how he had "been all right after the first couple of days." He spoke as if with amazement at his own inability to control his emotions immediately after her passing. This later became the first clue I ever had that my father was not comfortable with emotionalism or with closeness.

Several days after the funeral, my brother, father and I got into an argument about one circumstance or another of my mother's life and death. At length my father screamed at us, "You kids killed her! You killed her by your constant fighting with her!"

Chapter Eleven

Soon it was time for me to begin summer camp. I was driven to the campsite's location by the same kindly friends of my family with whom we had stayed when we arrived back in Baltimore from Ohio. While in camp that year, I was introduced to the world of still photography, a hobby which I took up and became quite good at over the next five years.

At the end of that summer, Susie and Billy were married in a service written largely by themselves. They exchanged vows in front of a Unitarian-Universalist minister at Rockford Chapel in Yellow Springs.

Susie and Billy received word they were both going to receive fellowships to do graduate work at Stanford University. Accordingly, they honeymooned to California, where they took up residence in married student housing on the Stanford campus. For the next three years in a row, I would spend my two-week spring vacations from Stockbridge with them at Stanford, flying back and forth each time.

Susie had been a Sociology major while an undergraduate at Antioch. Over the next four years she and Billy were at Stanford, however, Susie earned her master's degree in Communications, while Billy earned both his master's and doctorate degrees in English.

I returned to Stockbridge in the fall of 1968 and continued my education. My father remained overseas, while Gerson held down the fort in Arlington, Virginia, where we had moved from nearby Alexandria after Mom's death. Gerson eventually returned to school himself, then being free to do so. He graduated from Kent State University in 1973 with a degree in History. He has lived here in Baltimore ever since then and has worked for the Social Security Administration since then as well. In 1982, he returned to school to earn a master's degree in Transportation Planning five years later from Morgan State University. Gerson has never married.

The other students at the Stockbridge School were both predominantly affluent and already well-educated. As such, they were well prepared for the academic rigor the school offered. I felt socially inferior in many respects, something painfully reflected in my longing for a girlfriend.

In March of 1970, I went to California for what was then my second trip there during spring vacation. While there, Susie, Billy and I drove up to see a first cousin of ours on our father's side who was living in Marin County.

Previously, I had smoked pot several times before and felt I had had some pleasurable experiences while I was high on it. Therefore, when one of my cousin's roommates first offered me some marijuana, followed by some kind of potent hashish, I eagerly accepted. What I experienced for the next several hours was, at the time, the most terrifying experience I had ever undergone. This became my last contact with the world of drugs.

Chapter Twelve

My father had always wanted me to visit Israel and was willing to send me there. In the spring of 1970, he began a concerted campaign to persuade me to go. I had cited my need to stay home in order to earn the money to go to California again the following year. I had become dependent on my visits to Susie and Billy.

My father bargained with me that if I would permit him to send me to Israel, he would see that I would get to California the following spring. I relented because it was obvious how badly my dad wanted me to go. I also hoped this would be an opportunity for me to take many good photographs and, indeed, I did get quite a few.

I spent the first six weeks on an Israeli kibbutz, or communal farm. Here, I worked in the tomato and peanut fields at high noon, swam in the afternoons, and dined in the commune's dining hall.

Before returning to the U.S. at the end of the summer, I had an opportunity to travel around Israel, though I did so alone. I began by taking a bus north to the Galilee. I spent a weekend in the artists' colony of Safad, which was in the only part of the country that was at all mountainous.

Following that, I moved on to the ancient city of Tiberius, passing Capernaum along the way. Here, I stayed in an open Turkish tomb which had been converted into a noisy hostel. Directly across the street from the entrance to our hostel lay the banks of a heralded body of water.

I spent much of my first afternoon in Tiberius dangling my feet into the Sea of Galilee. Whenever momentarily I would hold my feet still, within seconds schools of small fish would gather around each foot to nibble at my toes. With the slightest movement of my feet once again, they would disperse in a flash, only to return, curious, once more.

Unlike the central and southern portions of the country, Northern Israel is humid in addition to being hot in the summertime. As a result, one perspires profusely.

I had taken precautions against the heat, but became dehydrated and mildly disoriented nonetheless. There happened to be a soda vending machine in the hostel, which I nearly emptied. I craved for another soda almost immediately after having finished the previous one.

That evening, though still disoriented, I decided to strike out in search of a restaurant listed in my tour guide booklet. I found the restaurant and after looking over the menu, decided on a good hearty steak and sides. Partially because I was still dehydrated, and partially because it had been quite a while since I had had any dairy products, I decided I would like nothing better than a cold, frosty bottle of milk to drink. Interestingly enough, the waiter initially brought me one.

The waiter knew I was a tourist who had simply forgotten about the local dietary laws. Nonetheless, when he brought my broiled steak, he grabbed what was left of the bottle of milk away from me. Scowling, he snarled, "This is a Jewish restaurant!" I didn't get the milk back.

That evening I tried, initially, to get some sleep on one of the ground levels of the tomb-turned-hostel. On either end of the tomb, buttresses jutted out which, in turn, led to open patio areas. Metal bunkbeds where people could sleep had been set up in each of these buttressed areas.

I lay down on one of these beds, but could get no sleep because of the noise. Wayfarers remained awake all night, talking, laughing and partying on the patios. Periodically, they would pass through our room on the way to and from these areas, and it was impossible to get any rest.

I was told there were more cots set up in the actual underground tomb area below and that, perhaps, I could get some rest down there. I climbed down the stairs into this area and located a long ovular stone chamber which was equipped with beds. This old tomb had been well restored, was clean, and was lit by lanterns placed intermittently along the floor. Seeking to get as far away from the noise upstairs and outside as I could, I chose the bed all the way at the end of this chasm, by the rear wall. Down here, however, there was no cross-ventilation whatsoever, and subsequently the heat was stifling. The mosquitoes were outrageous as well, and after ten whole minutes of being devoured, I gave up and reconciled myself to the fact I wasn't going to get much sleep that night.

I was 17 during this summer spent abroad and was beginning to feel the effects of depression without being aware of it. I longed to curtail my travels around Israel and return to the kibbutz where I had friends and where I felt more secure. I did so, and remained on the kibbutz the majority of the remaining time until we returned to the U.S. I did, however, have an opportunity to visit Jerusalem, the Tomb of Rachel, the Tomb of the Patriarchs Abraham, Isaac and Jacob, and the Church of Nativity in Bethlehem.

Thus, I can say I have stood by the spot where Jesus was born. On my way back from Tiberius, we had driven through Nazareth.

The summer had been well spent, and perhaps was even a little therapeutic. I returned home in a very relaxed frame of mind.

Chapter Thirteen

By the time of my senior year in Stockbridge, I had very subconsciously begun to worry about the fact I would soon be leaving my cradle of identity. Without having any understanding of why, I became severely and uncontrollably depressed. After a disastrous Christmas holiday, my family convinced my reluctant father he should pay for psychotherapy for me. Accordingly, upon my return to school I began periodic sessions with a former staff psychiatrist at the Austen Riggs Center who lived in the town of Stockbridge.

For numerous reasons, this was a depressing school year. In addition to what was taking place in my life personally, we had all witnessed a deterioration of the school's fabric. By my senior year, the drug problem on campus had become heinous. It became impossible to spend any weekend there without witnessing the bizarre behavior, at all hours, of students high on one or more types of substances. Vandalism of the school's properties and buildings became a serious problem as well. Due to numerous factors, Hans Maeder had lost control of the school.

While on my second trip to California, someone had given me a record album by Jim Morrison and the Doors that he no longer wanted. I took this back to Stockbridge with me and spent that spring trimester listening to it, becoming an avid fan.

A year later, in the spring of my senior year, I began listening to the Doors once again. I ended up running through the dormitory I was living in borrowing Doors albums from whomever I could in an effort to familiarize myself with their entire discography to date.

This was now the spring of 1971. The deterioration of the school mirrored, perhaps, the feeling of the world at the end of the 1960s and the beginning of the 1970s.

It was in the midst of this atmosphere of decadent anticlimax that I immersed myself in the Doors. One afternoon I heard for the first time a song called "Love Her Madly." I was highly attuned to the Doors' sound as a result of having listened to all their previous records. Though Jim Morrison's voice had changed and deepened since their earlier albums, I instinctively knew who had recorded this song. My reaction was almost symbiotic, and I immediately bought a copy of the new album on which the song appeared.

Still another factor that contributed to the intensity of this experience with music and poetry which I was undergoing involved another student named Warren Silenzi.

I don't believe Warren ever understood what my fascination with his appearance was all about. But, nonetheless, I came to realize that by way of his posture and style of dress, he personified to me everything the Doors were all about. Warren had an incredibly strong, machismo look about him which today can only be described as a cross between Burt Reynolds, James Taylor and Clint Eastwood rolled into one. This was long before I had ever heard of or seen Burt Reynolds. As a matter of fact, when I first saw Burt Reynolds on television some six years later, I said to myself, "That guy looks like Warren."

EX-INMATE IN EXILE

Warren Silenzi, who was 17 at the time, looked as though he was in his mid-thirties. Several years later, I took a series of photographs of him.

This fascination with my friend Warren's appearance can only be described within the context of what I was going through psychologically at the time. I had no understanding whatsoever of the fact that my experiences in boarding school, including my experience of listening to the Doors, had become a substitute identity for me after my mother's death.

A day or two before my graduation, Susie had flown in to be present for that day, though sans Billy. Gerson had flown up to New York from Washington in order to drive up to the Berkshires with Aunt Elyse from her house outside New York City.

Following my graduation ceremony, I was to drive back to Elyse's house with her and Gerson. After collecting my belongings, I went around campus saying good-bye to different people. My last stop before we drove off was the dining hall to say thanks and good-bye to the cooks. While I was in the kitchen, Hans happened to come in through the back entrance. I was pleased to see him and told him I would be leaving in just a few moments.

Hans looked at me, extended his hand, and grasped mine warmly in his. Giving me the warmest smile anyone has ever given me, and one which I will never forget, he said softly to me, "Good-bye, Philip."

In contrast to many other Stockbridge School students' relationships with him through the years, mine with him had been a close one. He was a mentor to me, and the education that I had gained from him over the previous four years has served me well ever since. Stockbridge was the inspiration that has enabled me to survive since then. To this day, I still dream of the school at night.

Chapter Fourteen

After boarding school, my father essentially gave me two suggestions (or choices) as to what I could do with the most immediate part of the rest of my life. I was desirous of going on to college, which, in the end, I was able to do. My father, however, balked, saying he either wanted me to join the Army or go back to Israel for a year. He thought I would swallow the idea of returning to the Middle East if he made it more delectable by compromising. I could go to school in Israel.

It's likely I should have considered myself lucky he did not insist that joining the Israeli Army would be a similar kind of compromise.

During the last couple of therapy sessions I had had with my psychiatrist back in Stockbridge, he and I thought we had uncovered the underlying reasons why I needed to see him in the first place. Thus, we erroneously concluded I would not be in need of psychotherapy any further.

Somehow or another, Elyse and I instinctively knew I had not seen the last of psychiatry. I, myself, did not feel secure enough to leave the United States, something which, in fact, I have not done since I went to Israel in 1970.

My father has always despised Elyse, and did in 1971 as well. Nevertheless, out of concern for me, Elyse steeled herself to do battle with my father in an effort to convince him to allow me to attend college in this country. Elyse won out.

EX-INMATE IN EXILE

In the midst of the demise of the Stockbridge School during my senior year, the faculty there had given us very little in the way of guidance counseling. Thus, not only did I perform miserably on the Scholastic Aptitude Tests, I failed to gain admission to any of the colleges I had applied to in the fall of 1970. One of the first favors Elyse did for me upon arrival at her house after my graduation was to take me to see the same person who had counseled all three of her children at Scarsdale Senior High School. This man was very friendly and very helpful. With his help, I selected three private colleges into which we estimated I had reasonable chances of being accepted. This time around, having finally some idea of what I was doing, I buckled down and applied myself to the business of applying to these colleges. I was accepted by all three, and I decided to attend Elmira College in upstate New York, my first choice of those three.

Not long at all after arriving back home in Virginia that summer, I discovered I wasn't through with the need for psychotherapy yet. I called my former psychiatrist in Stockbridge and asked him for a referral to someone in my area. He gave me the name of a doctor who practiced in Washington, D.C., with whom I established contact and began to see. My father was very annoyed to learn I still felt I needed help. Had it not been for Elyse's intervention once again, he never would have agreed to allow me to see this doctor even once a week. He became furious when he learned I was actually seeing this man twice a week.

What is astounding to me, retrospectively, is the degree to which I had no comprehension whatsoever of the root cause of my apprehension. I was still in the process of acquiring the tools of introspection at this point, and the idea that there could be some deeper reason why I was distraught was terrifying, as well as upsetting to me.

In addition to seeing my therapist each week, I took several courses at a nearby community college, my first introduction to the American higher education system.

The year following my mother's death, Gerson decided to finally proceed with the rest of his life. Though he had graduated from high school in Baltimore in 1961, he had had little opportunity to further his own education since then. In 1969, he was able to obtain financial aid to attend Northern Virginia Community College, where he completed two years of work. By 1971, he was ready to transfer to a four-year institution to complete work on his baccalaureate degree.

Gerson had been the only one maintaining the one-bedroom apartment in Arlington that we all used as a home/headquarters whenever any one of us was in the Washington area. As my father was still working overseas, it was necessary for us to break up house at the end of the summer of 1971, when Gerson was ready to transfer to Kent State University. Susie had been married for several years.

The very tense process of packing up our belongings, something which had occurred so many times in our family already, was torturous to me. Without understanding any of this, a major portion of my self was once again being torn out of me. Because we had lived in the Virginia area the entire time I had been in Stockbridge, the two locations were one in my subconscious mind.

In anticipation of leaving the area, I had terminated therapy with my psychiatrist in Washington. My father, who had come home to help us pack, had neither any understanding of, or concern for, why I was behaving the way I was, something he didn't hesitate to let me know. He thought my behavior was ridiculous. I had to practically beg him to allow me to attend one of the meetings of my old group therapy program, back at the Alexandria Community Mental Health Center. Without knowing it, I was wanting to use the A.C.M.H.C. as a crisis intervention resource. Though I was welcomed by Bill Taylor, who was still there, my desperate hope to find comfort and relief became illusory. I was astoundingly depressed.

We loaded our belongings into a rented U-Haul truck, said good-bye to the Washington metropolitan area forever, and drove to Brockton, Massachusetts, where one of my father's brothers was going to allow us to store our belongings for the next several years in some space he had for us. While in the Boston area, my father took Gerson and me to visit some distant relatives of ours before Gerson would have to depart for Ohio. I must have been a semi-pathetic sight, as these people took pity on me. They knew this boy was on his way down. My father neither knew nor cared.

By the time I reached Elmira, I was already in a substantially agitated state. It had been a number of weeks since I had last had a therapy session, and a tremendous amount of apprehension had built up inside me, which I needed to talk out. To compound matters, it took a number of weeks more for a therapist to be found for me in the Elmira area.

The day of my first appointment with a psychiatrist who had finally been located for me, I hurried to his office eagerly. I felt brimming over with a need to verbalize. But to my exasperation, this man would not permit me to operate in the same way I was accustomed to doing! Rather than allowing me to discuss what I felt a need to talk about, he kept insisting there was a more profound reason for my upset, a possibility I was not as yet ready to entertain. I was utterly stunned! Over the next several sessions during the next several weeks, I begged this man to allow me to discuss what I wished to discuss, but he refused. At length, he simply informed me he would not see me any further, and even threatened me with hospitalization. What was I to do?!

Elyse had, for a third time, talked my foot-dragging father into paying for treatment for me. As my father was still abroad, Elyse would initially lay out the money for my therapy bills, and then my father would reimburse her. As such, she had jurisdiction over my choice of therapists. Aunt Elyse's intentions for me were nothing but the best, but thinking I was simply being evasive in therapy, she refused to allow me to see anyone else, in what she thought was an effort to force me to confront myself. Night after night, beginning at midnight, I would call her collect from the pay phone on my floor in the dormitory where I was living. I would beg, scream and cry in my efforts to get her to allow me to see another therapist, waking everyone up and thoroughly disrupting dormitory life.

Not only was I in the midst of a terrible nervous breakdown, I nearly drove her into one as well. At length, I was taken to the emergency room of a nearby hospital and given an injection of a drug I had never had before called Thorazine.

By Thanksgiving of that year, I was no longer able to function, I was so terribly overwrought with anxiety.

Because of the state both of us were in, Elyse could not afford to have me at her house for that holiday as much as she would have liked to have done so. Instead, I was one of a handful of students who stayed on the Elmira College campus during this time. Because there were so few of us, the school was able to temporarily house all of us in one of their smaller buildings, thereby enabling them to close down the main dormitories.

It snowed heavily over this four-day holiday, and I was absolutely miserable, disheveled and worn-out. Walking aimlessly through the snow on campus, I would become catatonic for hours in the cold.

A day or two after the Thanksgiving holiday, several of the residential staff and the Dean of the school were able to talk me into going into one of the local hospitals voluntarily for a rest. I was on a regular medical unit rather than a psychiatric ward, but the Administration of the college knew I needed a rest which, indeed, I did.

While in the hospital, I discovered I had become a "mental patient" when a doctor came in to give me a rectal exam as part of the admissions process. He kept looking at me as though I was crazy as he stuck his finger up my ass.

While I was recuperating on the medical unit, Elyse was busy making arrangements for me to come to New York when I got out of the hospital in Elmira. Upon my discharge from the hospital, I packed up my belongings, said goodbye to Elmira College, and got on a bus to New York City. It would be some nine years before I would again set foot into any academic environment.

I simply wanted to return to Washington, D.C., to see the same psychiatrist I had seen during the summer. I had liked him and had felt he had been helpful to me. I was desperate to do this.

Elyse had most likely been planning on having me hospitalized once I got to New York anyway, even though she initially told me I could still go to Washington if I wanted to. The following day after I arrived, she took me to see her psychiatrist with whom she had made arrangements for me to be admitted somewhere there. He told me firmly he wanted me in a hospital. At that time, I was certainly unaware of any right I may have had to stay out of a hospital unless I chose to go in voluntarily.

A telegram was sent to my father, telling him it was felt I was in need of psychiatric hospitalization and a decision had been made to place me in such.

By this time, in spite of myself, I was beginning to see the futility of persisting with my wish to go back to Washington. I had been assured by Elyse's psychiatrist I would be amongst peers once I had been admitted to the acute psychiatric unit of Roosevelt Hospital on the west side of Manhattan.

This proclamation led me to believe the hospital would be a repeat of the Stockbridge School environment, and became, therefore, an intriguing form of coercion. Hoping to find a girlfriend on the ward, I agreed to go in voluntarily. Boy, oh boy, was that a mistake! It was also one I was to make on more than one occasion.

I remained on the ward for the full three month period of time still considered to be a short-term stay. I spent my first (though not last) Christmas in confinement. I was terrified being confined.

While I was there, I remained highly anxious, compulsive and catatonic. One staff member referred to my catatonic states as "posturing."

Initially, though medication was recommended, it was not forced upon me. One day, however, one of the nurses walked into my room with some pills in one hand, a loaded hypodermic in the other, and a big, burly West Indian aide behind her. She delivered her ultimatum, and as I hesitated, this West Indian aide psyched himself up to get tough with me and began trying to tear my pants off in order to expose my rear end. I had never been treated this way before and consented to take the pills orally. I pleaded with them not to give me Thorazine, as when I had had an injection of this in Elmira, it had given me the terrifying feeling of being high again as I had been in 1970 in California. I was given Stelazine instead. Stelazine made me sleep, and sleep, and sleep. The more I slept, the more I had need to sleep. My bones ached. As if oblivious to the effect this medication was having on me, I was punished by the staff for not being "willing" to participate in therapeutic activities on the ward. Again, I was never advised of any legal right I may have had to refuse medication.

Believing I had no other choice, I continued to take the medication. Medication was dispensed several times each day, and I was given mine each night before bed.

Eventually, I caught on to the fact I could put the pills under my tongue while under the staff's watch, and then spit them out a few moments later, something which I clandestinely did.

One night, however, I was discovered doing this. At that point, trapped, I dressed and managed to get on the elevator which was otherwise kept locked, preventing our escape. I didn't know where I was going to go, nor did I care. I simply knew that if from now on I was going to be faced with the threat of physical restraint and violence each time they wanted me to take medication I did not want to take, I could not stay. I have always found it fascinating that the decision I made to leave was referred to by the hospital as a decision to "elope." Can my readers believe this?!

The door of the elevator I had managed to get onto began to swing shut. I was on my way downstairs to the lobby of the hospital and to freedom.

All of a sudden, a staff member of the ward managed to jump into the elevator before the door had swung completely shut. He promised me if I would agree to return to the ward voluntarily, he would see to it I was no longer forced to take medication against my will. Being very relieved to hear this, I turned back. True to this aide's word, I was no longer force-treated.

It is most likely there was a reason why the staff member was able to evasively tell me he could "see to it" I was not treated against my will any further. There was probably a state law in effect which said I had the right to refuse medication so long as I wasn't considered to be dangerous. The difficulty is that, if this were the case, no one was ever honest enough, and possibly not lawful enough, to directly communicate this to me.

At length, I reached the end of the maximum three-month period of time still considered an acute stay in a New York psychiatric hospital. It was decided I was still in need of longer-term inpatient treatment, and because my father, tragically, had a super-duper insurance policy that would pay for all this, my family began shopping around for another institution for me. I remained unaware of the fact that I had a right to remain out of all hospitals unless I could be proven to be dangerous.

Several large, prestigious (?), private hospitals were considered for me to transfer to, including the Austen Riggs Center back in Stockbridge, Massachusetts, where I had gone to boarding school. Neither my family, nor my therapist, nor I were aware of the central role the Stockbridge School played in my downfall, and so Austen Riggs was chosen as the hospital I should next go to. For my part, I simply longed to go back to the Berkshires.

Austen Riggs is unique among mental institutions. It is known for its lack of formal structure. Here, there are no locked doors or seclusion rooms, and thus, the hospital does not take involuntarily committed patients.

It is a small hospital which had an inpatient population of only 40 people when I lived there. It much more closely resembled a large respite care program than any kind of traditional psychiatric hospital setting. Professor Erik Erickson, a well-known social psychologist, has done much research there.

Unbeknownst to me at the time, I was upset about many things which had already been unfair to me during that portion of my life I had lived thus far. I was angry at my mother for abandoning me by dying. I had already been subjected to, and thus frustrated by, my father's erratic personality. I was upset because I had never achieved the peer acceptance I had sought when a student at the Stockbridge School. And I still didn't know how to find the girlfriend I still longed for.

Medication was again offered to me, but again I declined usage of it. In therapy, I was not accomplishing much at all, though this was not at all due to any fault of my therapist. I, once again, had no understanding of the true basis of my dilemma and simply remained preoccupied with the trauma of my recent breakdown. Because I was subconsciously angry, I did not want to look at those same reasons why this was the case. Lastly, it is important to me that my readers understand that this entire psychological situation which I am describing was compounded by the mental impairment that I had. This is a phenomenon which makes it all that much more difficult to understand one's own motivations.

Unknown to me, I had placed myself in a very bad situation by wanting to go to Austen Riggs, where I would be so close to my old school, and yet so very far away as well. I began to divide the universe into two distinct halves: the past magical world of the Stockbridge School, and the rest of the earth.

In retrospect, it is now evident to me that in spite of the fact I had been given a schizophrenia diagnosis (I was 18 and 19 years old), I was suffering from depression as well.

This was the early part of the 1970s, when the remnants of 1960s counterculture were still abundant. I developed a fear, born of loneliness, loss of direction, and depression, of the intensity of 1960s life in New York City, with its then-netherworld of drugs and counterculture. I became terrified of this New York influence, though the city itself was some 140 miles away. I would refuse to eat anywhere except in my room, insisting all three meals per day be brought up to me on trays. I was afraid if I dared eat anywhere else except there, such as in a restaurant, someone else's house, or even in Austen Riggs's dining room, I would be "polluted" by New York City's long-distance intensity.

One weekend, in October of 1972, Susie and Billy came to visit me while I was at Riggs. They had, by then, left Stanford University and were in their first year at Cornell in Ithaca, New York. Having received his doctorate degree in English and Creative Writing at Stanford, Billy was now an assistant professor at Cornell. Susie had earned her master's degree in Communications at Stanford and was now working on her doctorate in American Studies at Cornell.

While Susie and Billy were visiting me in my room at Riggs that weekend, Billy inadvertently opened the window in my room several inches to get some air.

Because I was at such loose ends in life, I was desperately lonely and depressed, which made it excruciating to have to say good-bye to Susie and Billy at the end of this visit. After I had somehow managed to do so anyway, I returned to my room and found my window still open. This served as a desperate reminder to me of their visit, and I could not bring myself to close it, leaving it open instead for the next seven consecutive months. Graciously, the hospital staff did not insist I close it, electing to simply close the fire doors at the entrance to the wing I was in instead, thereby preventing the rest of the building from freezing off.

During this period of time, I stopped bathing or changing my clothes. Spoiled and dried-up food would litter my room until an attendant would come to take it away. When I slept, I would do so with my filthy clothes on, with the overhead light on above me, the door to my room wide open. I would cover myself with a coat.

At night, I would sneak out of a rear entrance to the building and roam the surrounding area. Frequently, I would become physically immobilized for hours on end in one spot somewhere.

I knew I was still on my way down in regard to survival. I began to become outrageously angry, though I exuded few external signs of this. I eventually began showering again, but would frequently become upset from the stimulus of the hot water while doing so. While under the water during these lengthy showers, my train of thought would be ambling along until I would stumble across some uncomfortable memory, which would trigger me off. I would escalate to the point where I would slam my fist against the wall of the shower stall. I was always amazed, though relieved, the staff never heard me. During these episodes, I would imagine dying in a hail of gunfire in a shoot-out with the police somewhere.

At other times when I would become suicidal, I would restrain myself by forcing myself to lie very still on my bed until my upset had passed.

I had long since stopped going next door to the medical office building to see my therapist. At one point, however, I informed one of the senior psychiatrists there, who had asked to see me, that I was having suicidal episodes. This man was definitive in his advising of me that he would have me transferred to a more secure setting if I truly lost control of myself. However, he did so in a very creative, warm, supportive and dignified manner, asking me if I would promise to come to him if I became very upset. I believe I did make this promise.

At length, the life force within me asserted itself, and I made a decision to live. Knowing, therefore, I had to extricate myself from the hell I had fallen into at Riggs, I began to realize it was time for me to move on.

The first therapist I had ever seen for individual psychotherapy was the psychiatrist I had begun seeing in the latter half of my senior year at the Stockbridge School. By 1973, this man and his family had relocated to the Boston area, where he was in private practice in Cambridge.

I decided I wanted to return to therapy with this person. I had learned of the existence of Maclean Hospital, just outside of Boston, and decided I wanted to transfer there voluntarily, where my former psychiatrist could obtain visiting privileges to see me. I was warned that Maclean was a very traditional institution where, were I to transfer there, I would once again be locked up. I simply wanted to get out of the situation I had walked into at Austen Riggs, of being so close to my old school without ever being able to be a student there again. And so, I did not listen when I was told I would once again be incarcerated were I to go to Maclean Hospital, voluntarily or not.

Chapter Fifteen

In June of 1973, I transferred from Riggs to Maclean, where I was promptly put on a locked ward. I was terrified being in this situation again, largely because I still had not made a determination to take advantage of the help available there. After merely one month, I requested to be allowed to leave.

Once while at Maclean, I was restrained by the aides and thrown in locked-door seclusion. While in captivity, I made psychic communion with Jim Morrison and the Doors. Several of the lines from one of the Doors' more notorious incantations, called "When The Music's Over," flowed through my mind comforting me.

I knew Jim wasn't with us anymore, but the belief on my part that if Ray Manzarek, Robbie Krieger, and John Densmore could have liberated me from this detention, they would have done so gave me courage, warmth and desperately needed inspiration.

The procedure by which a voluntary patient is released from an inpatient psychiatric facility at his or her request is probably a universal one. The patient is asked to submit a written notice to the hospital staff indicating they intend to leave the hospital within the coming 72 hours. During this period of time, a decision is made by the medical staff as to whether this person is considered to be dangerous either to himself or herself or to anyone else. If patients are considered to be dangerous, they can be further detained, regardless of whether they wish to leave or not.

EX-INMATE IN EXILE

I submitted my notice and was questioned at length by the psychiatrist who was the ward administrator. He asked me where I would go and what I would do if they released me. I told him I didn't know what I would do once I got out, but that I would rent a room in the nearest Y.M.C.A. so I would have some place to live. The doctor was concerned for me, but I was not dangerous, nor was I considered to be, so I was released.

My father was not immediately aware I was leaving the hospital, with the result that I had no money upon my discharge. My father had only recently retired to Bangor, Maine.

I took a transit bus into Cambridge and called my psychiatrist from a pay phone once I arrived. I told him my exact location, and he picked me up in his car. He drove me to the Cambridge Y.M.C.A. and lent me enough money to rent a room and buy food. He was later reimbursed for these expenditures by my family.

My father was by now aware I had left the hospital but balked at sending me any money to live on. Fortunately, Susie was able to talk him into doing so.

My father was never really concerned about what would become of me. I will acknowledge, however, that beyond that, he simply didn't know what to do with me, literally. For some reason or other, he came down from Maine to see what he could do about my circumstances, though I did not permit him to accomplish much. One day, on a crowded subway, he deliberately tried to lose me, partially out of idiocy and partially out of desperation. I caught up to him.

Several blocks from the Y.M.C.A. where I was staying, a first cousin of my father's happened to live. This was someone whom I had met several years earlier while still a student in Stockbridge.

This woman was very, very concerned for me, though she was ill-equipped to handle me. Out of concern for me she met with my psychiatrist to see what she could do to help.

My father despised her in much the same way he despised and resented Elyse. He had been verbally abusive to this first cousin of his previously, and when he found out she was trying to help me, he sent her a very rude and nasty letter which hurt her very much.

After a while, I was evicted from the Y.M.C.A., though at this point I do not remember precisely why. Fortunately, by then I had begun receiving income from my father, and so I was able to rent a room elsewhere. At this time, I did nothing during the day except wander. I saw my psychiatrist several times each week in his office. He was very warm and reached out to me, though I did not return the favor. I was accomplishing nothing in therapy, and was frequently in a foul mood.

Gerson had graduated from Kent State University in May or June of that year, had visited me once during my brief stay at Maclean Hospital, and had then gone down to Baltimore to look for a job there. He lived temporarily with the same family friends who had met us at the airport upon our return from Ohio when my mother had died, and who had driven me to summer camp.

In October, Gerson came up to Boston to locate me. It had been decided I should try living with my father in Maine. Instead of seeing my psychiatrist in Cambridge several different times each week, I would commute to

Boston once a week by Greyhound bus to have one lengthy session with him.

Gerson and I went by Greyhound up to Bangor. My father met us at the bus stop and we spent several days with him in his small apartment.

There was one afternoon where I must acknowledge the weather was very nice. My father wanted the three of us to take a walk through the Maine countryside. Hiking had always been a tradition in my family, emanating from my father.

My father wanted me to accompany him and Gerson, but I refused, wanting to do some writing instead. I was negativistic.

My father lost all patience with me. He walked over to me, wrapped his arm around my neck, and throttled me. As he pulled me by the neck off the chair I was sitting on, he lost his own balance, and we both ended up on the floor. And still he didn't relinquish his grip on me. Instead, he dragged me by the neck, inch by inch across the room. I nearly lost consciousness.

It was only after he had me completely out of the house that he let go of me, beat a hasty retreat back inside, and locked the screen door behind him to keep me out. It is good he did this, as had I been able to get back into the house, I would have killed him, and I told him so. My father did not believe in telephones and thus had none. Instead, he dispatched Gerson to summon the police. Gerson had done nothing this entire episode except stand around and watch. He was only too happy to go and get the cops.

When two Bangor police officers arrived, they found me halfway up an available ladder I had leaned against the side of the house. I was attempting to gain entry through a window.

It was only then my father unlocked the screen door and came outside. He immediately told the police he wanted me committed to a mental institution. They informed him they couldn't do that, but told him in my presence that if he felt he was having any more problems with me he should call them back, and this time they would take me away. With that, they left. Neither my father nor Gerson ever advised them that I was the one who had just been severely assaulted and battered. It was not going to do me any good to try to convince these officers of this, as they were not going to listen to any wild-eyed kid with shoulder-length hair and a chest length beard whose father had just finished asking them to lock him up.

My father ordered me to leave first thing in the morning. I was permitted back inside just long enough to get some sleep before getting on a bus to go back to Boston.

Chapter Sixteen

Eventually, I found another room, this time not far from Harvard Square in Cambridge. I spent my time sleeping, wandering and hitchhiking across the Charles River to Boston. I began spending a lot of time in the student library at Boston University, as well as elsewhere in the student union building, where the library was located. While visiting the library, I was able to read an entire biography of the Beatles without needing to check it out. This was the second Beatles biography I had read in my life.

I would frequently listen to music in the record listening room of the library. In general, I enjoyed the academic ambience of the university. During this period, the Watergate controversy swirled around Richard Nixon. One night while watching television in the student union at B.U., the news came on the air that Spiro Agnew had resigned the vice-presidency.

In proximity to Thanksgiving that year, I called Susie and Billy long distance in Ithaca and asked them if I could come to their house for the holiday. Susie hesitantly told me that, yes, I could come, but I couldn't stay for more than a few days once I got there. Overjoyed and tremendously relieved, I hitchhiked from Boston to Ithaca, New York.

Once back in Cambridge after Thanksgiving, I returned to my routine of sleeping, wandering around the Boston area, and spending quite a bit of time at Boston University.

I did not wish to be alone for the approaching Christmas holiday, so I called Elyse and asked her if I could spend Christmas with her. She said no and begged me not to come. I went anyway.

On Christmas Eve, I boarded a bus late that evening bound for New York. As we entered the city, I congratulated myself. I was now entering the same New York City of which I had been so terrified not so long ago while at Austen Riggs.

Since the last time I had visited Elyse, she had sold her house in Scarsdale and had purchased a condominium on Park Avenue in Manhattan. I arrived on Elyse's doorstep at approximately 1:00 a.m. on Christmas morning, against her wishes. Elyse felt she had no alternative but to allow me in.

Elyse fed me and allowed me to get some sleep on her guest bed. She allowed me to spend Christmas Day with her and her guests before insisting I leave in the afternoon.

After leaving Elyse's house, I again found myself stranded. I called the father of one of my old classmates from the Stockbridge School, who himself was a good friend of mine and remains so to this day, and who also lived in Manhattan. I asked him if I could come and stay with him and his wife, and they consented out of considerable kindness. They could not care for me, however, and after several days they felt forced to ask me to leave as well.

By now it was New Year's Eve. As a child, I had many times watched the famed descending of the illuminated ball down the side of the old Allied Chemical Building in Times Square in the midst of the festivities hosted by Guy Lombardo on television.

EX-INMATE IN EXILE

Having absolutely nothing else to do, I decided to actually *be* in Times Square that night, though I was to discover what a bad decision this was.

As can be seen on television, Times Square is absolutely mobbed on New Year's Eve, regardless of the weather. I jockeyed my way around in the crowd until I reached a point from which I had a good view of the perched ball. It was odd watching the ball slowly descend at midnight without the familiar voice of the television announcer as he counted down. All that happened this time was that a roar went up from the crowd as the ball reached the end of its journey. It was cold and raining, and I was homeless and miserable. I began to cry.

The crowd was raucous and packed shoulder to shoulder. I was simply waiting for a fistfight to break out, knowing damned well a stampede would ensue if it did. Fortunately, this did not happen.

I was carried along by the crowd as far as 38th Street before I was able to move of my own volition. I continued on down to 34th Street, where I took up residence at the Pennsylvania Railroad Station beneath Madison Square Garden.

I learned from another homeless peer that if one descended onto the platform level of the station, one could sometimes get some sleep in the seats of darkened and idle passenger cars on nearby tracks. I quickly discovered, however, it was necessary to sleep with one eye open, proverbially speaking, within this arrangement. One had to be on the alert for movements of the train, unless one wished to wake up and find oneself in the midst of some vast and darkened train yard somewhere. It's entirely possible train crews deliberately jostle these cars around periodically in order to flush out potential vagabonds, such as myself at the time. If so, their strategy works. This is an absolutely lousy way to attempt to get any sleep.

Another family of old friends of my family was a man, his wife, and their children who lived in Montgomery County, Maryland. Lately, I had become close friends with the oldest son, who had recently graduated from Brown University in Rhode Island. Bob was now living in New York and was working in the real estate business. Bob had once come to visit me while I was in Roosevelt Hospital.

After several more days and nights of living and sleeping in 34th Street Station, I called my old friend Bob, who was concerned for me. He told me to go ahead and come up to his apartment, and he and his roommates would see what they could do to help me. When I arrived at his location, he let me in, fed me, let me use his shower, and allowed me to get some sleep on his couch.

Bob had been raised in the Reform tradition of Judaism, but had later converted to Orthodoxy. The following morning, Saturday, Bob normally would have attended worship services at his synagogue. Instead, he escorted me down to the Port Authority bus terminal and made certain I boarded a bus for Boston. Just before I got on the bus, he gave me a sealed envelope, with strict instructions not to open it until I had arrived in Boston.

I could not bring myself to return there as, under the circumstances, there was simply nothing there for me whatsoever.

As my bus backed out of the bay into which it had pulled, I saw Bob waiting determinedly until I was out of sight. Immediately after we had emerged from the underground tunnel which exits the Port Authority building, however, I asked the driver to allow me to get off, which he did.

Bob had been a very good friend to me, I knew I had betrayed him, and I was disappointed with myself for having done so. I did not feel I had any other choice at the time, however. Sadly, I opened the letter he had told me not to read until I was back in Boston. Bob knew I had many friends in the New York area, and his note said once I had established myself in Boston I could feel free to stay with him whenever I wanted to visit these friends in New York. He would not, however, participate any longer in my being homeless.

At this point, I do not recall what precisely enabled me to return to the Boston area, though I did eventually return. I returned, somehow, to my listless life there, void of direction.

Chapter Seventeen

I did, however, discover the location of the Jewish Student Union building on the urban B.U. campus, known as the Hillel House. I felt welcome there at the time and began attending informal, student-led worship services on Friday evenings. Though I had never kept kosher before, I was able to purchase kosher meals there for a very reasonable amount. I did so on several occasions. I spoke on one occasion to a rabbi there and told him of my troubles. Sadly, he was unable to do anything more for me other than to acknowledge the desperation he heard in my voice.

At length, I began wanting to return to the Baltimore/Washington area. I had pleasant memories of weekends spent in Boston while a student in Stockbridge. But beyond this, Boston was not home to me. My thoughts began ambling back to my early childhood in Baltimore. I decided if I were going to be doomed to wander streets aimlessly, I would prefer to wander ones which were once familiar to me. I was also still making a connection in my mind between the Washington area and my experiences in the Stockbridge School.

I had no idea where I would live when I arrived in either Baltimore or Washington. Sylvia and Tookie had by now both retired and had moved back to Baltimore where they had both been born and raised. Gerson had been living and working in Baltimore for several years. But I had no idea whether anyone would consent to allow me to live with them or not. What enabled me to make a definite decision to migrate was our former maid, Ruth, now retired. I knew even if all else failed, Ruth would never permit me to be forced to sleep in the streets.

I left Boston on the day of my 21st birthday, February 25, 1974. Susie and Billy had given me permission to come to Ithaca again, in honor of this birthday. Again, I hitchhiked.

Susie and Billy permitted me to stay an entire week with them this time before they supportively, yet firmly, insisted I leave. Billy was supportive and philosophical, though he speculated neither Gerson nor Sylvia and Tookie would allow me to live with them, were I to arrive in Baltimore.

On the day of my departure, I boarded a bus bound for Boston which began winding its way east across New York State.

By the time I reached Syracuse, however, I felt compelled to disembark. I got off the bus and called Billy back in Ithaca, desperately hoping he and Susie would permit me to return there. Again, Billy was supportive, but firm in their resolution that I must not return to Ithaca. He urged me to continue on to Boston.

After hanging up the phone, I felt completely stranded, psychically. Literally having no place to go, I hitchhiked into the center of Syracuse from the outlying area where the Syracuse bus station was located. I spent several hours wandering aimlessly around downtown Syracuse, at one point getting evicted from the lobby of an office building I had wandered into.

At length, I hitchhiked back out to the bus station and decided to call my psychiatrist in Cambridge. I did so from a phone booth immediately outside the bus station.

This bus station was located in one of the seedier neighborhoods of the city. As I spoke over the phone, some thoroughly inebriated bum came stumbling up to the phone booth I was in and began beating on the door, insisting I let him in. This event struck me as an astounding mirror-image of my own destitution.

I finally boarded another bus and headed east again. I had decided I wanted to go back to see the old Stockbridge School campus once again that I had thought of so very many times since the last time I had been there. In Albany I got off the bus I was presently on and took another to Pittsfield, Massachusetts. From there, I hitchhiked the rest of the distance into the town of Stockbridge.

Upon arrival in Stockbridge, I began wondering where I was going to sleep. I ran into an old acquaintance of mine from when I had been a patient at Austen Riggs. He invited me to spend a few days with him and his roommate, which I did. Following that, I spent several more nights on the floor of the room of one of the other patients at Riggs, who remembered me from when I had been a patient there, and who had since transferred into the halfway house.

Following this, I was once again at a loss for a place to sleep, most immediately.

While I had resided at Austen Riggs, I sometimes would visit a drop-in center program which had been started for the benefit of the local teenagers in town. This drop-in center met on the second floor of the rectory of the Episcopal church, located in Stockbridge.

I had heard the key to the rectory hung on a nail on the back porch of the priest's house, also located on the church's grounds. I found this key, and each night I would steal onto his porch, take the key, and let myself into the rectory. Though I would hide my small, old-fashioned suitcase within the rectory somewhere, I would sneak out of the building early each morning before anyone else came in. Without being seen, I would replace the key and hope I would be able to do this again the following evening. It was only March, and one night it snowed heavily while I was upstairs in the rectory.

One afternoon when the rectory was open anyway, I went in to try to retrieve my suitcase from the location I knew I had hidden it in the night before. To my dismay, it wasn't there, and I suddenly realized I was in trouble. Sheepishly, I identified myself to the church's priest and asked him if I could have my bag back. He informed me, sternly, that he had turned it over to the town police.

At this time, the Stockbridge Police Department consisted of four sworn officers and two cruisers with radios in them. Their headquarters were located in the Stockbridge town hall, down the street from Austen Riggs. Their office consisted of one large fluorescently lit room with a lone cell in one corner.

I decided to go down and face the music for having burglarized the Episcopal church's rectory.

When I got there, no one seemed to be around, though the office was open. No one was presently residing in the cell either. I did happen to see my suitcase sitting in one of the other corners, however, and so I thought I would simply take it and ski-daddle on out of there, which is exactly what I did.

By this time, it was beginning to get a little warmer, making it feasible to sleep outdoors. Aziz, the person on whose floor I had slept at Austen Riggs's halfway house, lent me a sleeping bag so I could at least keep warm wherever I ended up flopping. For the next number of weeks, I slept in open fields and surrounding forests.

There was a laundromat in the town of Stockbridge that had a utility closet in it. I was aware of what time the laundromat was closed up for the night, and so when it was raining, I would hide in this closet. After the owner of the business had closed everything up and left, I would emerge from hiding. No one would know I was inside, as the owner of the laundromat always pulled the shades down before leaving.

During these incidences of my being in the laundromat and the church rectory, I was vaguely aware I was doing something very wrong by being on these premises illegally. At the time, however, I was desperate enough to do these things anyway. While living in Boston, I had opened a bank account after my family assured me my father was, by then, willing to deposit modest amounts of money into the account each month for me. While wandering around in the Stockbridge area, I would go to the town bank and ask them to advance me money against what was in my account in Boston. I would then sign whatever papers were necessary in order for the Harbor National Bank to reimburse the Berkshire Bank and Trust company for the money they had given me. Thus, I had money to eat with, but not enough to rent a room anywhere.

Several months after I graduated from the Stockbridge School, Hans Maeder retired. Earlier in the year, a search had been conducted for a successor to him. A new director was hired who headed the school for the next several years before he departed. An alumnus of the school was then hired who became the third director.

I had always remembered how one night when I was in bed in the dormitory I lived in while a student at the school, I had had an odd dream. For some peculiar reason, the idea of sleeping behind the stage in the school's gymnasium had an appeal to me. Now seemed like a real opportunity to live out my fantasy.

When I first began showing up on campus, soon after my arrival in Stockbridge, the director of the school initially tolerated my presence. At length, however, he became impatient, and informed me that in view of the fact I was no longer a student there, I was no longer welcome or wanted.

The entrances to the school's gym were never kept locked, and one night I went in to try out my fantasy of many years ago.

The following morning, a student found me asleep behind the stage and reported me to the director, who was irate. Upon finding me there he ordered me to retrieve my suitcase and get into his car immediately, which I did. He then drove me off campus. I was very frightened that he was going to take me to the police and pleaded with him not to do this. Either he had not been planning on doing this in the first place, or else I succeeded in changing his mind as we rode along. Fortunately, he simply deposited me on Main Street in town. This was the last time I saw the old school.

The Chief of Police in the town of Stockbridge was Officer William Obenhein, affectionately known as "Officer Obie." Obie had gained fame and notoriety when he played himself as the arresting officer in Arlo Guthrie's downfall, in Arlo's satirical 1960s cult film *Alice's Restaurant*. I had become friendly with Obie while at Austen Riggs, introducing myself as another alumnus of the Stockbridge School. Arlo had likewise been an alumnus of the school, though he had graduated before my tenure there.

After several more days of vagrancy in town, I finally enabled myself to leave Stockbridge and continue on with my journey to Baltimore. I left on April 30, after two full months in Stockbridge. I had arrived there in the dead of winter. I was leaving in the spring.

It is quite obvious to me that had I remained in Stockbridge any longer, I would have seen the inside of that sole cell in the Stockbridge police office in town hall. Most likely because he was aware of my activities around town, but also possibly because he was frustrated at the ease with which I had removed my suitcase from their office, Obie told me to either shape up or he was going to lock me up.

Chapter Eighteen

The night I finally left Stockbridge, I stood for over an hour in the pouring rain in front of the tollgate entrance to the New York State Thruway in West Stockbridge, Massachusetts. West Stockbridge borders on the New York state line.

At length, I got a ride to New York City, which left me at the entrance to the Holland Tunnel at 3:00 a.m. Just after daybreak, I got another ride which deposited me along the highway out in the New Jersey flatlands. Here, I was astoundingly lucky I wasn't struck and killed by any one of the tractor-trailer trucks that flew by me. These would go by so quickly the accompanying prevailing wind was nearly enough to topple me over.

I got still another ride, which took me to the Port Authority railroad station in Newark. I had just enough money to purchase a one-way ticket on Amtrak from Newark to Baltimore. I arrived in Baltimore on the afternoon of May 1, 1974.

Upon my arrival in Baltimore, the first thing I did was call Gerson from the railroad station. Gerson did not sound terribly surprised to learn I was in town. He told me to go ahead and get into a cab and come out to his apartment. He would pay my fare when I arrived.

After we had sent the cab on its way, we went inside and began to talk. Gerson seemed to know of my hope to go and live with Sylvia and Tookie, though he was uncertain as to whether they would consent to this or not.

Several days later, we both went to their house so the four of us could discuss my circumstances.

Tookie seemed to have lost the sense of humor we had thought he had as children. He and Sylvia were adamant and steadfast in their refusal to allow me to come and live with them. At length, Tookie picked up my suitcase which I had brought with me. Opening their front door, he placed my suitcase in the hallway of the apartment building they lived in. He then pronounced derogatorily, "There are all your worldly possessions -- in a cardboard box," and ordered me to leave.

Because I still had not, as yet, committed to rehabilitating myself, I also found it impossible to commit myself to getting any place of my own to live in. Gerson permitted me to store my belongings in an outside closet which contained his air-conditioning unit, but otherwise he, as well, ordered me out.

I had known if all else failed, which all else did, I could always stay with Ruth, and I did stay with her. But Ruth was elderly by now, and even more alcoholic than she had been when she was our maid. She could not care for me, and I could not stay there. I left.

Homeless again, I hitchhiked over to the Washington area and was permitted by the parents of an old friend of mine in Alexandria to stay with them temporarily. This family lived immediately in back of the same high-rise apartment building we had lived in at the time of my mother's death. This was the same building Sylvia and Tookie had moved to after their sale of the house they owned when I was a child. I had spent most of the summer of 1971 with them here, after Gerson and I had begun fighting too much for me to remain with him in Arlington.

And so, this building was a central figure in my mental connection with the Stockbridge School experience.

One evening, I had gone into this apartment building to use a pay phone I remembered was located in one of the ground floor hallways. While I was on the phone, a highly confrontational maintenance man who did not know me questioned me as to what I was doing in that building. Intimidated, I began arguing with him, and the police were called.

When the Alexandria police arrived, they were equally confrontational. We argued for several minutes before they gave me an ultimatum to leave. When I foolishly refused, something occurred that had never happened to me before. I got arrested.

I was taken to a precinct headquarters, booked, and charged with disorderly conduct. Fortunately, I had enough money on me that I was able to immediately post bail and leave.

Even before this night, I had had a mild fear of the police. I had drifted further and further towards the fringes of a normal lifestyle, though this had not been my own fault. As I did so, however, I began to become wary of the police wherever I was. Being arrested for the first time, an experience akin to rape, severely intensified my fear and hatred of the cops and the entire legal system. These are feelings which I continue to struggle with to this day, albeit to a lesser extent than I did back in the 1970s.

I felt I had to be "unarrested" somehow, and if this could not be done, I would commit suicide. Little did I know this was an experience I was to undergo several more times before I would be done.

EX-INMATE IN EXILE

After my release from the detention area of the police station I had been brought into, I ran straight into the police officer who had arrested me, in the hallway. I begged him to "unarrest" me. He looked down his nose at me, laughed in my face, and simply told me to speak to the city attorney who would be prosecuting me.

After this escapade, I returned to the house of my friend's parents, who had long since gone to bed, but who had left the back door open and the kitchen light on for me. Though it was very late by now, I felt the need to talk to someone.

The Washington metropolitan area had at least one crisis intervention hot line number in operation, and I called it. A voice came on the line and asked how they could help me. With this, I began pouring out my soul. After perhaps 20 minutes of an admitted diatribe on my part, I suddenly became aware of a slow, rhythmic sound on the other end of the line. Listening a little more closely, I realized I was hearing snores. My counselor was truly fast asleep.

The next day, I went to see the Alexandria city attorney, who turned out to be a man named Burton Handberry.

I pleaded with Mr. Handberry to allow me to be "unarrested," which he refused to allow to happen. He questioned me as to how I had come to be arrested, however, and I told him truthfully of my entire set of circumstances.

I was vaguely aware that I should perhaps see a lawyer somewhere about all of this, and told Burton Handberry so. Somewhat surprised, Mr. Handberry informed me that he, himself, was an attorney. Pleasantly surprised to hear this, and not understanding the difference between the defense and the prosecution back in those days, I began peppering him with questions as to how the hell I could get out of this mess. In the end, Burton Handberry agreed to simply dismiss the charge against me when I appeared in court.

I spent the summer of 1974 drifting back and forth between Baltimore and Washington. When I was in Washington, I was initially permitted to stay in a dormitory at Georgetown University. I was in Washington at the time Richard Nixon resigned the presidency.

When September rolled around and students began to arrive for the school year, I was still staying in the same dormitory I had spent most of the summer in, although I realized I was now going to have to leave. At length I did leave but, of course, found myself with the same perennial question then of where next to sleep.

One night while pondering where to flop, I found myself standing immediately outside the entrance to another of Georgetown University's dormitories. The door to this building was locked from the outside, but as I stood there, a student came down some inside stairs and exited the building. Perhaps thinking that I, myself, was a student there, he held the door open for me to enter, which I did. I located a lounge area on one of the floors and went to sleep there on the furniture.

The following morning, I was still asleep in the lounge area when the fire alarm went off, though this later turned out to be a false one.

Tired, I foolishly did not get up to exit the building like everyone else did, remaining there sleepily instead. Suddenly, two plain-clothed officials from the fire marshal's office came in and discovered me lying there. They immediately asked me who I was, what was I doing there, and how had I gotten into the building. When they found out I was not a student there, they immediately took me into custody and escorted me to the campus police headquarters. From there, the District of Columbia police were called and I was taken away.

When we had lived in Baltimore, in the comfortable neighborhood we were in before we left for Santiago, Chile, there was a warm family down the street from us named Borinsky. David Borinsky was the first truly close friend I had ever had. David was one of three boys and three girls, "The Borinsky Bunch" they called themselves, Selma, Lou, and their six children.

David had a very warm and kind older brother named Daniel to whose wedding, in 1969, I was invited and thoroughly enjoyed. Daniel had attended law school, and he and his newlywed wife, Susan, settled down not far from us in Northern Virginia.

After I had been booked, charged with unlawful entry, and taken to the D.C. City Jail, I had an opportunity to make phone calls. I called Dan who, along with his wife, was very concerned for me. He told me he would do everything he could to get me out of jail.

I spent my first night in jail and was then taken to the District Court the following morning. Because the charge of unlawful entry carried a potential jail sentence of one year, I was entitled to representation by a public defender. A gentleman was assigned to my case, who then interviewed me. While in the basement of the courthouse he questioned me as to how I had come to be in the situation I was in.

At length, he advised me to enter a guilty plea, telling me I was then still young enough to be placed under a youth probationary act.

When I did enter my guilty plea a while later, the presiding judge then asked me how exactly I had come to be arrested. I was unable to tell him.

I felt a tremendous sense of perverse relief. I felt that at last I had sunk to the bottom of the barrel and from here on in, things would simply have to look up for me. Since I was unable to account for how I had gotten into the situation I was in, someone else was going to have to.

Daniel had posted bail for me, and I was released. He then drove me to his and his wife's house in the Virginia suburbs. I was to return to court to be sentenced the following day.

When I appeared in court in the morning, my public defender was once again there for me. To his surprise, the judge sentenced me to a year's supervised probation. At the completion of my period of probation, the record of my conviction would be expunged.

The judge had been aware I had been wandering around the northeastern U.S. He was also aware I had a history of mental health problems and had most recently been in treatment with a doctor in Cambridge, Massachusetts. Beyond this, he didn't know what to do with me. My attorney speculated that by placing me on a supervised probation, rather than an unsupervised one, he would be certain I would get the psychiatric treatment I needed.

I was ordered to begin probation immediately and told of where to report to, to meet my probation officer. When I did meet with him, he told me efforts were being made to contact my psychiatrist in Cambridge. He also gave me permission to go over to Baltimore at my request.

I went back to Baltimore, but as always, struggled with the problem of where to sleep. Gerson, Sylvia and Tookie were all still refusing to allow me into their homes. I ended up simply lying down in the grass behind one of the buildings in the apartment complex my brother lived in.

I lay outside and found myself thinking of the extent to which my life had deteriorated. And suddenly as well, as I lay there, I began to become aware of some other unidentifiable change taking place within me.

I didn't understand what was suddenly different inside me. I didn't understand I was finally, *finally* deciding I had incurred enough trauma in life. Consequently, I didn't understand where adjoining feelings of relief, hope, and minimal security were coming from either. What I did know, desperately, was I needed these feelings to remain. The extent to which the impairment I still have befuddled me now astounds me.

I got up from the grass and decided to look for the nearest laundry facility belonging to the apartment complex. If necessary, I was prepared to sleep on top of the machines. When I found an open laundry room, I went in and scouted around. In addition to the laundry equipment, there was a series of wire storage stalls, assigned one to each apartment in that building of the complex. Finding an open, empty one, I simply crawled in, curled up inside, and went to sleep on the floor.

In the morning, a woman came in to do her laundry, discovered me asleep in the storage area, became terrified, and called the apartment complex's security guards. When they arrived, they ordered me out into the open where they detained me until the police arrived. It is unlikely that if I had run away any kind of all-points alert would have been sent out for my apprehension, simply on the basis of my having been found sleeping in a laundry room, albeit illegally. Nonetheless, out of some bizarre sense of duty, I stood there cooperatively, fully aware the cops were coming to lock me up again. Facetiously speaking, they didn't have to charge me with resisting arrest.

After being booked and charged with trespassing, I was taken to the County Jail, where I was permitted to make some phone calls before I was put into the general population for the night. I called Susie, collect, and asked her to wire me enough money to post bail. She agreed to do this, though she informed me my father had instructed her not to, were I to ever call and ask her to do so. I also called Daniel Borinsky in Virginia, who came over to see what he could do to help me again.

The following afternoon, the money Susie had sent arrived; I posted bail and was released. From a pay phone outside a convenience store I called Daniel in Virginia and gave him my exact location. He, in turn, called a friend of his in the Baltimore area and asked him to come pick me up.

Having finally made a commitment to myself to better my life, I had simultaneously enabled myself to commit to getting a room of my own to live in. Daniel's friend, Len, drove me downtown to the Y.M.C.A. and advanced me enough money to rent a room.

I had been frightened that I was going to be in serious trouble with my probation officer in Washington, D.C., when I informed him I had been arrested again in Baltimore County. Fortunately, he was not terribly concerned since this was simply another manifestation of my inexplicable homelessness.

When I appeared in court, I entered a plea of "nolo contendere," an agreement whereby the record of my conviction would again be expunged, in exchange for my admission of guilt.

At length, I received a note from my probation officer in Washington saying my probation there had been terminated. Most likely, the court had received the information concerning me they had requested from my psychiatrist in Cambridge. He had probably recommended they dismiss the charge against me, and they had decided to do that.

Chapter Nineteen

In December of 1974, I relocated from Baltimore's Y.M.C.A. to the Albion Hotel, also in the downtown neighborhood. In the 1970s, there were still a number of cheap flophouse hotels downtown where one could rent a room for perhaps $25 per week. It has been the disappearance of these cheap places to live since then that has resulted in Baltimore's homeless population.

I spent my time wandering, visiting with friends, watching television, and listening to music. Later on, after having been sent by my family to Sheppard-Pratt Hospital, I was to realize the extent to which I had been enjoying this life devoid of responsibility.

I knew, however, my life of leisure was leading me nowhere, and I did wish to move productively on. One night, I made a horrendous effort to get the help I wanted and now understood I needed. I still was not taking any kind of medication at the time, and thus, putting one foot in front of the other for a distance of some four or five miles took an incredible effort. But I had made up my mind to get help, and there was no turning back now.

I had called Directory Assistance and informed the operator I needed the phone number of the nearest location I could go to for crisis intervention. She gave me a particular phone number, which I then called. I explained my predicament to the person who answered the phone. This person was supportive and gave me directions as to how to reach their location. In the middle of the night, I walked from the Maryland Institute, College of

Art, through the entire length of Baltimore's Mount Vernon neighborhood, through the downtown commercial district, and into the Federal Hill neighborhood of South Baltimore. Here, I located what today is known as the Carruthers Clinic.

When I arrived, I was let in by a man named Fred who may have also been the person to whom I had spoken over the phone. Fred could see I was highly wrought up, and he spent several hours talking with me supportively. In the context of his talking with me, I agreed to go with him voluntarily to the emergency room of Johns Hopkins Hospital in East Baltimore. Fred told me he had notified the on-call psychiatrist there I would be coming in.

When I arrived at Johns Hopkins, the on-call psychiatrist was busy with someone else. I waited impatiently for an hour or more. While I waited, I also noticed this Baltimore City cop hanging around in the E.R. When I went to ask an attendant nurse how much longer it would be before the psychiatrist would be coming out to see me, this cop decided to glower at me. Completely spooked by this, I decided I had no intention of hanging around any longer under these circumstances. My hatred of the pigs was such that I decided to leave. Ironically enough, the on-call psychiatrist emerged just in time to see me turn and wave good-bye, as I backed out the door. He stood, literally, with his foolish jaw hanging wide open.

I had given the Albion Hotel as my address. Presumably, this information had been passed on to other sources, as several days later, someone from a community mental health center called me. This person was supportive and urged me to get the help I needed. I had had enough, however. I no longer felt safe getting help in Baltimore, where I had had problems with the law.

One night in May of 1975, I went to visit a newly found friend and spent the entire night talking with this person. Just after daybreak, I left this person's house and went to get a ride home. I stood hitchhiking on one of the main thoroughfares in Baltimore. As I stood by the side of the road waiting for a ride, I noticed an intriguing side street I hadn't ever realized existed before. It was lined overhead with alternating branches from trees on either side of the road. Large, elegant, secluded homes were perched to one side in this affluent North Baltimore neighborhood. I decided to see what lay at the end.

I walked down this very pleasant road, in the quiet of the early morning air, enjoying the scenery immensely.

I came upon a house set back from the road which had a driveway leading up to it. I do not recall whether there were any "No Trespassing" signs posted or not. If there were, I did not see them.

I made the mistake of walking up this driveway, which turned out to be a private one. I had only wished to get a better view of the house. Apparently, however, the family living in this house decided to call the cops.

Suddenly, three patrol cars and two paddywagons materialized out of nowhere, lights flashing and sirens screaming. Suddenly realizing I had done something wrong, I returned voluntarily to the curbside. I was immediately surrounded by a half dozen cops, one of whom began arguing, and arguing, and arguing with me. This one in particular demanded to know what I had been doing on private property. I told him I had not been aware that was what I was on and apologized for having been on such. Nonetheless several of these cops continued for the next 45 minutes to make every effort they could to intimidate and provoke me. The owner of the house never did me the courtesy of coming outside to confront me, even in the presence of the pigs. I was told I would be arrested if I were found on any of the streets in that immediate neighborhood again. I was then told to turn around and leave, which I began to do.

I knew, however, I had not deliberately trespassed. I also knew so long as I didn't enter any private driveways, they had no right whatsoever to tell me I couldn't be seen on any particular public street. I told them so over my shoulder as I walked away.

Suddenly, I found myself thrown up against the back of one of the cop cars, my hands forcibly twisted behind me, and handcuffs placed around my wrists. In the ensuing 45-minute provocation session leveled at me after these rear-ends initially arrived, most of them had disbanded and dispersed. But now they were called back again, a paddywagon arrived, and I was placed inside. I had become the most recent victim of Baltimore's long history of police brutality. My family, however, was later to take great glee in pronouncing this incident to have been due entirely to my "long hair" and "beard."

I was taken to the precinct station where I was led into an office. While I sat in a chair, still handcuffed, some young black pig walked in and placed his gun on the desk. Feigning establishmentarian civility, he announced to the world (I was the only one there) what a great cop he was since he had never had to use that weapon.

I had mentioned in the course of all this that I had been hospitalized for mental illness. Thus, after I was booked and charged with disorderly conduct, I was transported to a short-term forensic unit which had been established in one of the public hospitals in Baltimore City, rather than to the City Jail. There I spent the night before appearing before a panel of officials the following day. When I did appear, I was questioned at length about what contact I had had with the mental health system in Maryland. I told them of my visit to the Carruthers Clinic, and of my brief involvement in a transactional analysis group, though this had not proven helpful. At length, I was told I was going to be released from there and that I would not have to appear in court. I was warned, however, that if I were arrested again, it would be seen to that I was court ordered to a state hospital.

Chapter Twenty

One day while back at the Albion Hotel, I received word from my family that Elyse's daughter, my cousin Margie, was to be married. My entire family, including my father and I, was invited to the wedding in New York.

I had not abandoned my intention of getting psychiatric help, though I was no longer willing to look for that in Baltimore. I began making plans to use my upcoming trip to New York as an opportunity to get some of that help.

I went up in time for the wedding and sat with my immediate family, including my father, through the ceremony and the following reception, which were pleasurable. A day or two following that, all the guests who had assembled in New York except me, returned to their respective corners of the earth. At that point, I entered a five-month period of homelessness in New York City once again.

I had constructed elaborate plans about where I wanted to go for help, though in retrospect, I realize these were completely unrealistic. I wanted, ultimately, to return to Boston now to get help but first would need to return to Baltimore to collect my belongings. The difficulty was that I was still very upset and angry about everything, with the result that I had to struggle within myself constantly, particularly as I was still not taking any kind of medication at this time. As a result, I simply became catatonic and stranded in New York.

I once again began making a series of phone calls, in an effort to find out what mental health resources existed in Manhattan. I was eventually referred to a crisis intervention clinic located in a tenement building in a Puerto Rican neighborhood on the upper Westside. The staff of social workers who operated this clinic were warm and reached out to me. Because of my circumstances, I was not able to appear for regularly scheduled appointments. As a result, I would have to wait until my customary counselor was available to see me each time I arrived. But I was very willing to do this, and this person would always spend an hour talking with me subsequently.

I spent many weeks sleeping in Riverside Park, gazing across the Hudson River to New Jersey during the day. I would sleep behind a row of bushes in front of the New York Public Library, located at 5th Avenue and 42nd Street. One night while asleep behind the bushes, I awoke to find some guy screwing his girlfriend against a bank of floodlights aimed at the facade of the building. And, of course, I slept in Central Park.

At one point in my talks with my counselor at the crisis intervention clinic, he told me of a special program located in Greenwich Village called "The Door." This was a program funded by the city of New York which served as a psychosocial program for anyone who was homeless in the city. It turned out to be located in what was once a vast department store. A shelter or other residential arrangement to which I could have been referred was connected with the primary program. I agreed to look into this program voluntarily, and my counselor at the crisis clinic notified the program managers I was coming down.

When I arrived at "The Door," there was a uniformed guard at the entrance who terrified me, though he was harmless. I permitted myself in past him only because I was intrigued to see what the entire program looked like. I also felt welcomed by the staff.

I was greeted by a social worker who led me to an intake area which had been cordoned off from the rest of the vast floorspace. As she interviewed me, she ordered a special high-protein drink for me from the kitchen, made of flavored raw egg yolks.

After I had been interviewed, I was permitted to wander through the rest of the building to discover all that was offered there. I was intrigued to find that photography and woodworking were available, among other activities. Complete shower facilities were on the premises as well.

As I was exploring the facility, I came across a young, bearded man who introduced himself to me. This person was friendly and outgoing, and I was therefore surprised when he informed me he was a psychiatrist. I wanted very much to remain at this program, as there was a tremendous amount of opportunity offered here. I also felt very welcome. But I was still very upset there was a uniformed guard at the entrance.

I knew I had to reach out and verbalize to someone how I was feeling about the guard at the door, so I trusted in this friendly psychiatrist. He told me, supportively, they had a guard simply because they had recently had problems with the local Hell's Angels. He told me he would be happy to introduce me to the guard.

We walked over, and he told the security guard my name. This person was no one more than an elderly, semi-frail black man. Other than his uniform and badge, his only accoutrement of intimidation was a nightstick. He smiled warmly at me, and extended his hand. I grasped it haltingly.

Knowing still that I needed to reach out more to others in order to get the support I needed, I approached a young woman who was, like me, a client there, and put my trust in her.

Sadly, she was not at all sympathetic or supportive. She simply dictated to me that as far as she was concerned, this program had much to offer. If I were to leave, as I felt the instinct to do, I would simply be "cutting off my nose to spite my own face."

This was more than I could bear. As I left, a large group of people had joined hands in the middle of the floor space and were dancing in a circle as a gesture of community. I absolutely hated myself for leaving and remain convinced that had I not encountered this confrontational woman, I would have stayed. But at the time, I could not stay, and so I bolted out the door.

The social worker who had done the intake on me saw me leaving and chased after me. Catching up to me, she implored me to return, but I was too upset. I left.

Chapter Twenty-One

One day I fell asleep on a park bench in Greenwich Village and woke up several hours later. I had had a beautiful dream about my mother.

Chapter Twenty-Two

At length I received word from Elyse, whom I had stayed in contact with by phone, that my father was coming to New York to try to locate me. She told me when and where he had said I could meet him, and this was where I did find him.

My father told me he had come to New York to locate me and place me on a bus back to Baltimore. Later on he was to tell me he genuinely felt sorry for me when he saw how forlorn, dirty and homeless I was. That evening, we went to a cheap steakhouse, and he bought me a steak dinner. In my mind, this remains one of only two times in my life when my father was genuinely compassionate towards me.

The following day, my father did put me on a bus to Baltimore.

While in New York, I had wanted to be able to leave in time to be in Washington, D.C., for the Fourth of July. Something appealed to me about the idea of being in Washington for Independence Day the year immediately before the Bicentennial. Thus, I was exceedingly frustrated I was not able to mobilize myself to leave at that time.

And so, I developed a kind of obsession about going on to Washington, to simply *pretend* it was still the Fourth of July, even though this was now the month of November. Thus, when I did reach Baltimore, I got off the bus only long enough to put my suitcase in storage. I then went on to D.C.

EX-INMATE IN EXILE

I became physically stranded in Washington, D.C., of course, for an additional six weeks, by which time it had become very cold. Though I was unaware I had taught myself how to meditate, it was only through the use of breathing techniques that I was able to loosen myself up enough to return to Baltimore.

Upon my return to Baltimore, I discovered I would be unable to get my old room back again at the Albion Hotel. Instead, I took another room at another hotel.

This period of time spent on the streets of New York had been peculiar. In spite of the physical discomfort of being dirty and homeless, I was not devoid of hope. I knew one year earlier I had turned a critical corner. It was now a matter of struggling against my own hostility.

In the beginning of February 1976, I borrowed a television from a friend to watch the upcoming winter Olympics. I had discovered the Olympics as a child and enjoyed watching them every four years.

Like everyone else, I first saw Dorothy Hamill as she marched in the opening ceremonies. And like everyone else, I was taken in by her perky, pixie-like presence. Over the next two weeks, I tracked her path to glory in her winning of a gold medal for figure skating. Dorothy seemed the picture of perfection, prosperity, success and security. These were all qualities I now felt desperately hopeful of acquiring for myself.

Because I was reading all these things into her, I developed an obsession with her, probably similar to the one John Hinckley developed in regard to Jodie Foster. These are agonizing feelings which drag on for years before they mysteriously disappear.

EX-INMATE IN EXILE

I never stalked Dorothy, though, ironically, I believe I passed her on a street in Georgetown in Washington, D.C., several days after the Bicentennial.

Chapter Twenty-Three

In April of 1976, I was one of several people evicted from the hotel we were living in, then known as the Abbey. The management of the hotel was, however, courteous enough to make alternative arrangements for us to live before they booted us out. I relocated to the Alcazar Hotel.

I had taken to sleeping during the day and being active at night, a pattern which I continue to this day, and which is not unusual for people who suffer from depression.

Early one morning in August, I returned to my room at the Alcazar after having been out all night. I was readying for bed when there came a knock at my door. I opened it to find one uniformed police officer, accompanied by a plain-clothed cop. They asked me whether I was Phil Kumin or not, and when I replied that I was, they told me to come with them. I enquired as to what was going on and was told I was wanted for questioning at police headquarters in regard to a fire that had occurred at the Alcazar. Initially I had no idea whatsoever what they were talking about.

I was not immediately arrested and was not, therefore, placed in handcuffs, though I was transported to headquarters in a paddywagon.

Upon arrival at police headquarters I was taken upstairs where I was questioned for perhaps 90 minutes. I was told someone had burned a T-shirt on a stairwell I myself frequently used to get downstairs. Suddenly, I remembered I had seen some soot marks at the base of the wall on this stairwell, though I was not responsible for having put them there.

During the course of my discussion with my examiners, I made the mistake of mentioning I had been previously hospitalized for mental illness. At that point I was immediately presumed guilty, was handcuffed and formally arrested and charged with arson. I was taken to the same forensic unit I had been sent to a year earlier, this time to be evaluated for my competency to stand trial. As it appeared the only reason I was arrested and criminally charged was because I had talked openly about having been hospitalized psychiatrically, I was relieved when I was found to be competent. This, I thought, would be the end of this entire mix-up. To my dismay, however, I found I was not going to be released simply because it had been determined I was competent and had not set any fires as a result of having been psychotic.

Instead I was transferred to the Baltimore City Jail, where I spent the next 4-1/2 weeks in captivity. During this time, my family hired an attorney to represent me. Although a reasonable amount of bail was set, which my family could have afforded to pay, both my family and my attorney gave me the rationale that "it would look better to the judge" if he or she could see I had had an opportunity to post bail but had elected to stay in jail anyway. As upset as I was at the time, it did not occur to me I would have looked much better in the judge's eyes if he or she could see I had had an opportunity to jump bail but that this was what I had not done.

When I was finally taken to court, my attorney, for one reason or another, asked the presiding judge to delay my case until I could be more thoroughly examined forensically. He then asked the judge to send me to Springfield State Hospital for a 30-day examination, which the judge agreed to do. When I was returned to court again at the end of this period of time, my case was merely dismissed for lack of evidence. It is clear to me now this entire episode was what my family and my attorney thought would be a way of "teaching me a lesson." This was their way of telling me they thought I wasn't moving fast enough towards achieving productivity.

On October 25, five days after I had finally been released from this entire legal fiasco, I went in voluntarily to the Sheppard and Enoch Pratt Hospital, though at my family's insistence. I strongly suspected my right not to be falsely accused or illegally detained had just been violated in the previous two months of incarceration. As a result, I contacted the Maryland chapter of the American Civil Liberties Union and spoke with the then-Legal Director there. This person urged me to put a complete description of the affair in a letter to them, which I did. Several weeks later, however, I was told by them either they did not believe I had grounds for a lawsuit against my family, the state, and the attorney who might have misrepresented me, or else that the ACLU could not take my case under any circumstances.

Chapter Twenty-Four

Initially, after my admission to Sheppard-Pratt, I continued to resist the usage of medication. But nonetheless, I have a very vivid memory of lying awake in bed one night. I was thinking how happy I was to finally be somewhere I believed I could get the help I needed and was now ready for.

The psychiatrist I had as an inpatient at Sheppard was, indeed, a friendly man in his own way. He had a sense of scruples about him as well, which was more than I was ever able to say concerning the different doctor I saw as an outpatient at Sheppard. Though I was completely unable to articulate this at the time, the difficulty with my inpatient psychiatrist was that he had an astounding flat affect of his own. This, in combination with his complete avoidance of the usage of any counseling skills whatsoever, made me feel it was impossible to converse with him. Thus silence reigned supreme in his office during the entire year and a half that I was an inmate there. On numerous occasions I requested a change of therapists, but was never granted such by the hospital.

Immediately before Christmas that year, I decided I did not want to remain in this hospital and wished, instead, to return to my previous life in downtown Baltimore. I submitted the customary 72-hour notice informing the hospital I wished to leave by the end of that time.

Sheppard-Pratt is this astonishingly elitist, opulent and silly cross between a country club and a looney bin. In order to remain so, there is a tremendous profit motive involved in keeping individuals there as long as can be done so the hospital can continue to collect those people's insurance money. Thus, it is not surprising a decision was made by the hospital to see whether they could have me committed against my will to their institution, bogus though this effort turned out to be.

The customary two psychiatrists were called in from outside to evaluate me for eligibility for involuntary commitment. The first one, bald and arrogant, informed me he was going to fill out the necessary papers for me to be certified. The second one informed me he was not going to do this. As a result of only one of these doctors certifying me, but not both of them, I was free to go.

Unlike when I had left Maclean Hospital, my father had been notified in advance of my plans to leave. Thus, I received a telegram from him just before I would have left saying if I did leave, he would not send me any money to live on. Because I was frightened of living completely independently, with Social Security benefits as my only source of income, I felt compelled to retract my statement of intent to leave. Merry Christmas.

Shortly after New Year's, I was provoked by the hospital staff into adverse behavior. This then gave them the excuse to seclude me against my will (which was done), consider me to be dangerous (which I wasn't), and then medicate me against my will. I took the medication for the period of time I was told I had no choice in the matter. At length I was told I no longer had to take any medication if I did not choose to continue to do so.

I continued to take the medication voluntarily anyway. Several months later, the hospital decided to withdraw me from it experimentally to see how I would respond. I discovered then that, with the exception of side effects incurred, I felt much better on medication than I did without it. I have taken medication of one kind or another consistently since then.

The worst side effect I experienced from the drug I was on, one called Mellaril, was horrendous sedation, so much so that I could hardly get out of bed in the morning and had no energy whatsoever during the day when I did. Again, as had been the case in Roosevelt Hospital, the staff deliberately held me responsible for my inability to wake up, and insisted I was being "uncooperative." A daily ritual evolved whereby the head nurse would assemble an entourage of several muscle-bound male aides. She and her goon squad would then march into my room, uninvited, and inform me if I did not get out of bed, the mattress I was sleeping on would be flipped over, and I would be dumped on the floor. When they would then follow through with this threat, a fight would naturally ensue. They then had the perfect excuse to throw me into seclusion again, consider me dangerous, further medicate me (this time against my will), and threaten to have me involuntarily committed if I decided to leave the hospital at that time.

One of the worst aspects of being locked up in a mental institution, particularly an opulent, private one such as Sheppard-Pratt, is that one is thrown in with other people, many of whom come from entirely different backgrounds than one does oneself. Thus, we are forced to interact with people with whom we would never normally choose to associate. As Sheppard-Pratt is an entirely affluent environment, I felt socially ostracized not only by the staff and administration of the hospital, but by the other patients there as well. Each time there was a confrontation between myself and the staff there, I was made to feel as though I was being treated the way I was because I didn't have $100,000 in either pocket at any one given moment.

My father came to visit me twice while I resided at Sheppard-Pratt. On one of these visits in particular, he was astoundingly hostile towards me.

In January of 1978, my father received notification from his insurance company that they were going to begin limiting the amount of coverage they offered for mental health services. Going by Sheppard-Pratt's prices, we estimated there would only be enough money available to pay for inpatient treatment for me into the beginning of June. When June did finally roll around, I made a planned for, sudden and stunning recovery and was discharged. When I emerged from this looney, looney bin, I was in a very bizarre situation. I was improved in that I was now using medication, which I had found to be helpful. But after more than 19 months of being persecuted on the ward, I was even more demoralized, and thus suicidal, than I had been at the time I entered this stinking place.

Chapter Twenty-Five

When I was discharged, I was finally given the change of therapists I had been denied as an inpatient, since my inpatient psychiatrist was leaving the hospital. The doctor who agreed to see me as an outpatient had no flat affect of his own, and, thus, I did feel I could converse with him, at least initially.

When I was discharged from the inpatient service at Sheppard-Pratt, I was discharged to a state-funded psychiatric halfway house known as Hamilton House. I was once again in the downtown neighborhood of Baltimore where I had been living prior to jail, Springfield State Hospital and Sheppard-Pratt.

Initially, my plan for daily structure was to attend a day treatment program five days per week, participate in an evening program two nights per week, and see my therapist. I carried out this regimen dutifully for the first six months after my discharge.

I had wanted to go out and get a job for quite some time, as a source of income of my own was something I had never really had. Tookie, by this time, had taken a part-time job as a technician in his retirement. He worked for a medical film company in the Baltimore area owned by another long-time friend of our family.

One day, Sylvia informed me Tookie had spoken to the owner of the company about giving me a part-time job, and he had decided to offer me one. What had held me back from getting a job was the terror of being fired. But I wanted to work so badly I decided to take the risk of losing my job anyway. I've always been very, very pleased I did this. I began working two days each week and gradually increased my days at work while correspondingly decreasing my attendance at the day treatment program. Within a year, I had achieved full-time status at work.

By June of 1979, I was ready to leave Hamilton House. By August, I had located my own studio apartment. The first I had ever had, it was still located in the downtown Mount Vernon neighborhood of Baltimore and was therefore within walking distance of Hamilton House. I moved in on the first of September that year.

I have always felt Hamilton House was one of the few mental health resources I have ever benefitted from. Though not all of the staff were specifically trained in counseling or human services, all were supportive, and I gained as a result. The then-director of the House was quite pleased with the progress I had made while living there, as was I.

There developed more and more difficulties between my outpatient psychiatrist at Sheppard-Pratt and myself. I was expected to be at work at 8:00 a.m. at the film company, which was located a 40-minute bus ride from where I lived. As I have never had a car or a license to drive, it was necessary for me to get up very early in the morning to get to work on time. This, in turn, was impossible to do because of the same horrendous sedation I incurred from the medication I had to take as I had experienced initially in the hospital. While on this drug, Mellaril, I would sleep from 14 to 16 hours per day on weekends when I didn't have to get up. Although I would be in bed by 10:00 or 11:00 p.m. the night before, typically I would not be able to wake up before noon or 1:00 p.m.

the following day. At that point, I would simply jump into my clothes without shaving, bathing or eating. As there was no bus service to the location where I worked during midday, I would have to jump into the first cab I could get and spend $12.00 riding to work. I would be terrified I was going to be dismissed from my job the moment I walked in the door. Although this didn't happen until 1983, I was forced to endure the scorn and ridicule of my co-workers, including that of my own Uncle Normand.

I would walk into my psychiatrist's office and complain repeatedly I couldn't get out of bed in the morning and that I was terrified of losing my job as a result. I had no idea whatsoever I was suffering from sedation, as I was never told of this. Instead, this doctor would simply insist I "try harder" in the morning. Doctors routinely do not inform patients of potential side effects of medication they prescribe for them because of fear on their part that if they are truthful with them, their patients will no longer take the medication the doctors know they need.

Another ongoing matter between my psychiatrist and me was the abuse I had received while an inpatient at the hospital. I was even less able to accept the unfairness of what had been done to me back then than I remain today. Today, I understand the fact that my psychiatrist worked for Sheppard-Pratt himself, and this was why he would not acknowledge any wrongdoing on their part, represents a "conflict of interest" in legal terms. At the time, however, I had no understanding of this concept at all. I was simply naive enough to trust my doctor.

My doctor used to love to laugh at all of these problems I suffered from so badly. Once, realizing I was on the verge of suicide, he retreated just a little and admitted to me "it had been reported" there were rights violations taking place on the unit I was on at the time I was there. When I pressed him for more specific information, such as names of specific staff involved, he laughed in my face. "Mr. Kumin," he sneered, "you don't expect me to tell you *that* do you?!" He knew damned well I did.

Another time, I threatened to bomb Sheppard-Pratt. Laughing again, he sneered once more and told me that if I were to do that, I would wind up in prison, and Sheppard-Pratt would simply be rebuilt.

It was next to impossible, psychologically, to escape this torturous environment. The hospital uses the most subtle of means to ensure patients remain emotionally dependent upon it. One is lured by the beauty of the grounds, which beckon to a life of prosperity, impossible to obtain so long as one remains trapped there. Sheppard-Pratt, however, retains the opportunity to control you, while simultaneously bleeding either yours or your insurance company's pocketbook dry. It is a false dead-end.

Chapter Twenty-Six

In March of 1983, I lost my job at the film company. It is ironic that within a year after I had begun this job, a state law went into effect which could have protected my right to work as a disabled employee. It might have done so by mandating that "reasonable accommodations" be made for me on the job in order to enable me to carry out my responsibilities effectively, and thereby remain employed. In the case of my job at the film company, I could have used this law to insist my employer give me my own 24-hour access to the building where we worked, thereby enabling me to determine my own hours under the circumstances. It is not at all definite this law would have been properly enforced in my behalf, even if I had known about it. There was also a federal law which had been in effect ever since 1973 that might have accomplished the same thing for me. But no one had ever told me of the existence of either of these laws, or where to go to attempt to implement them.

While living at Hamilton House, I spent Christmas of 1978 with Susie and Billy in New York. By then, they had left Ithaca. Susie was now teaching at the Queens College of the City University of New York. Billy was now at the State University of New York at Stonybrook on Long Island.

Round about this period of time, Susie and Billy both decided they had had enough of me and my problems, none of which they had ever really understood, or believed in, though they had given me the benefit of the doubt for many years now. Additionally, my father was wreaking havoc on their married lives together, much the same as he had done to mine on an individual basis. One of the inspirations Susie and Billy's marriage to each other had held for them was an opportunity for Susie to escape the stupidity and hell we had been through as children. They were not happy to discover they had not left these realms yet. Lastly, they both had their professional teaching careers to be concerned with as well.

While I was with them in December of 1978, Susie and I got into an argument about one thing or another one night. Billy initially tried to stay in the background as Susie and I argued. Naturally, he felt protective of Susie, however, and at length he lost his patience. He screamed at me, "Fuck you, Philip A. Kumin! Either shape up or ship out!"

Even before I left my job at the medical film company, I had begun to wonder what I wanted to do with the rest of my life, vocationally speaking. I did not want to be earning only minimum wages indefinitely. In the summer of 1980, I enrolled in a music literature course at Towson State University, followed by an introductory sociology course in the fall semester of that year. I paid for the cost of these two courses out of my own pocket, as my father had made it clear he no longer intended to pay for my college education. These two classes also constituted my return to the classroom for the first time since 1971.

I also made a decision to undergo vocational aptitude testing and evaluation, and I contacted the Maryland Division of Vocational Rehabilitation accordingly. The only thing I was aware of being interested in at the time was music, although I also knew in my heart I was not proficient on any instrument.

I underwent a battery of tests, the results of which were sent to a Jewish career counseling service here in Baltimore. At length, I was asked to come to a group workshop meeting which focused on finding one's purpose in life, and hence, which directions to go in vocationally.

When I arrived in the waiting area of the counseling service on the appropriate day, there were already a number of other pending group participants assembled. One woman in particular, appearing to be either in her 20s or 30s, sat with an entirely bored and obnoxious smirk upon her face. Approaching her, I attempted to make inane conversation by asking her how she had come to be involved in this program. She replied one of the rabbis at the synagogue she attended had referred her there. I then asked what kind of work she was currently doing, and she told me she was an attorney. At that, I mentioned I had always been confused about the difference between a civil law case and a criminal one. Her way of replying was simply to pronounce that what sometimes begins as a civil case can become a criminal one.

We were called into the meeting room, and the workshop facilitator began by stating that to have an understanding of what kind of career to consider going into, one had to be a "directed" person, psychologically speaking. She then went around the room and asked each participant to talk about what things were "directing" them in life. When she came to our young female attorney, this woman started off by saying it shouldn't be very difficult for her to find a new path to follow, considering how directed *she* was. She then went on to articulate her list of accomplishments in what must have been her most polished of grandiose ways. She was fairly dancing around, she was expending so much energy in her efforts to be as repugnant as she could possibly be. I was absolutely stunned by the display of obnoxiousness exuded by this Jewish cunt purporting to be a lawyer.

My treatment in general, at the hands of the Jewish community in Baltimore, had not been much better. Years earlier, while walking through Jewish neighborhoods, I might encounter some miniature and archaic Jewish lady and her mate out for a stroll. They would squint and view me through nothing more than the slits of their eyes, during the entire length of their passage around me.

To this day, my brethren do not understand that there has been more than one Holocaust this century. They do not understand that this one has taken place right here in the streets and mental institutions of America. Here in Maryland, we have three regional concentration camps: one called Springfield, another called Spring Grove, and a third called Crownsville.

In fact these are they, my brethren, who constitute the vanguard of the latest round of executioners.

In the end, it was mutually agreed upon by both the Division of Vocational Rehabilitation and myself that the results of my aptitude tests had not given me enough to go on at the time. I was still uncertain of what I wanted to do. There was some talk of D.V.R.'s being willing to pay for a limited number of additional psychotherapy sessions for me. At length, however, I was told for the time being my case would be closed. I was advised, nonetheless, I would be more than welcome to reestablish contact with them at a later date, should I desire further guidance.

EX-INMATE IN EXILE

In 1980, while I was still working at the film company, I decided I wanted to take a vacation and go visit a first cousin of mine. I was, by then, working full time and felt, all things considered, I owed myself a vacation. I decided to accept an invitation from Sylvia and Tookie's son, David, to come and visit him and his family for a few days. David lived in Minnesota, and I looked forward tremendously to my trip to and from there by train. I planned to use my own money to make this trip, not any my father had given me.

I had recently begun to understand the difficulties I had caused my father and others during the decade of the 1970s and had written him in an effort to apologize for this. In this letter, I made the mistake of telling him I was thinking of going on vacation the first part of 1981. I received the following reply, dated October 6, 1980:

Dear Philip:
  I was upset by your recent letter, not only because you resent my advice, admonitions and efforts to curb your idiotic way of life and call them crap, but you are as stupid as ever about the spending and saving of money. Your behavior has improved a lot since you started working, but in such things as travel and long distance phone calls, you are little different from what you were 12 years ago.
  You resent my "crap," but you don't mind dishing out your own brand about your "love for me" and your "determination to enjoy a good relationship with me." What magazine article did you get those phrases out of? I doubt you even

know what they mean. And I know you offer them only on your own terms, since you reject everything I suggest.

I don't want words from you, promises and bleats about how hard you're trying, etc. If you want my love and a good relationship, give me some good performance; make me proud of you. When you do well and your boss acknowledges it with a raise, I am very happy and I raise your allowance. If you should ever get an A in some tough substantial course given by an honest teacher, I would be happy about that too. But when **you** tell me you are intelligent, I say **bullshit**. I know from your performance and your behavior that you have a head made of cement. Don't kid yourself. You had trouble all through grade school. You barely made it through high school. I know because I saw you in class and I was disgusted. I spoke to your teachers and they were disgusted. You managed to get into a third rate college and washed out after two months. You are now having a hard time with the courses you are taking in night school. What makes you think you can ever get a college degree?

You say you are hardworking and love your job at the film company. If so, why can't you get up in the morning and go to work? Is it that you are lazy and prefer to lie in bed and dream about being a superstar singer? How often do you clean your apartment? Why don't you cook in your apartment and save the money you spend on eating out?

EX-INMATE IN EXILE

You say you are honest. But you never hesitate to lie to me and to others. You never hesitate to make long-distance calls and charge them to other people. You are always ready to chisel a free meal from someone, or get the psychiatric treatment you are hooked on, at someone else's expense, if at all possible.

You say you are concerned. About what? That you can't get something for nothing? So far as I can see, that's the only thing which concerns you. Are you ever concerned that if you should lose your job you would have a hell of a time getting another because you have no skill and would be competing against thousands of other people who have no skill for the few unskilled jobs available? Suppose your boss should die of a heart attack and the company dissolved. Are you ever concerned that no girl who was any good at all would want to marry a jerk who earned barely enough to support himself when he worked, and had no savings of his own?

I urged you to go to vocational rehabilitation (against your will as usual) to get help in determining your aptitudes, and to learn a skill so you could earn a better living. What happened? You come up with great glee about a scheme you apparently concocted to have them pay for additional psychotherapy. How will that help you earn a better living when it hasn't after 10 years of treatment for several years of which you had five full sessions a week? How stupid can you be? Don't you recognize the reality of your situation? You are nearly

EX-INMATE IN EXILE

28 years old. You can only do the most simple kind of work. You can't even type. You are irresponsible and don't have any money despite your earnings and the $250 a month I send you because you spend it as fast as you get it on the most trivial and ephemeral of things. You dream of being a big shot, rich and powerful, and you dream of being cared for by a kind, motherly woman. What are you doing to achieve all this?

You point out that you have $652 in your savings account which you earned. You didn't save that voluntarily. It was "forced" savings [quotation marks mine --P.K.], money the insurance company sent as reimbursement for the money you spent on doctor's bills. The $500 certificate originally came from my money, not what you earned. Just see how cock-eyed your thinking is. You say you plan to spend the money on:

A trip to Minneapolis	$350.00
A trip to California	500.00 min.
A sofa bed	400.00
A record player	100.00
A vacuum cleaner	<u>25.00</u>
	1375.00 minimum

You don't even have half that amount! And how are you going to pay for your doctor's bills, school tuition, and all the rest of the things you want? I tried diplomatically to dissuade you from the Minneapolis trip. You said NO, you are going because you had never been there. Gentle hints and kind words make no impression whatever on you. Only sledge hammer blows to your block head have any meaning, like being locked up in the quiet room in the hospital, handcuffed and thrown in jail by police or being beat up by bums. Since this is how you are, this is what I shall do:

I am ordering you not to make those trips to Minneapolis or California.

If you disobey me, don't bother to call or come to see me when I come to Baltimore. I want nothing more to do with you.

As soon as I find out you have made either of the trips, I will not give you that $500 certificate.

I will immediately cut off all the Aetna and Medicare insurance you get under my policy and for which I pay. You can pay your own medical bills without reimbursement.

These are some of the things I can do and which I **will not hesitate to do** if you continue to regard me only as a source of annoying crap and a patsy to be milked.

DAD

Though this was, by far, the worst letter I had ever received from him, this was representative of the kind Susie, Billy, Gerson and I (among others) had always had to contend with from him. When my mother was alive, she would regularly have to endure these postal assaults whenever it was necessary for her to plead with him overseas to send enough money for all of us to live on.

At this point in my life, I was feeling better and better as a result of my own accomplishments. I was getting sick and tired of receiving these filthy, derogatory letters from him in the mail and told him so. I received the following reply, dated March 21, 1982:

Dear Phil:

Several weeks ago you sent me a 12 page letter, the first half of which was nice and pleasant and the last half full of angry gibberish. I ignored the second half, thinking it was a temporary aberration. Yesterday I received four pages of idiotic crap. Here is my answer.

You have a fart in your head. I have no intention of falling on my knees to kiss your shitty ass every time you regally wave your hand and bellow, "I want your respect!" Your actions and letters show you have no idea whatever of the meaning of love and respect.

For 25 years you have ignored my suggestions and disobeyed my orders. Yet you want my love and respect. You are touched by my present and don't remember ever receiving one before. You chose to forget the clock I gave you several years ago, which I don't recall your ever acknowledging, the $90 driving course I gave you while you were at Stockbridge, and which you flunked, the skiing lessons, etc., and on and on and on. Yet you **demand** my respect and loudly proclaim your love for me. In the language of your associates, "Go take a flying fuck for yourself." So much for that....

We continue to receive letters of this kind from him to this day.

Chapter Twenty-Seven

Our former maid, Ruth, had been living in retirement for many years because of gradual loss of her ability to work, in turn due to health problems and old age. We remained in contact with her, and she with us, nonetheless. Periodically, she would call Susie, Gerson and me and ask us for money, which we were only too happy to give.

After many years of trying, in 1981 Ruth was able to obtain better quality housing for an amount she could afford to pay. Gerson and I helped her move into a centrally air-conditioned, one-bedroom apartment located on a ground floor level, for which she paid $96.00 per month in rent.

As Gerson went with several other people to retrieve the last load of Ruth's belongings from her old place, I sat with her in her new bedroom and learned things about her then I had never known before. In a drunken stupor, she talked about her childhood in Accomack County, Virginia. She talked about the different families she had worked for before she came to work for my mother. She talked about how my mother had always counseled her to "put money aside" and how she had done this. The last time I saw Ruth, she had passed out on her bed, television on and blaring at the foot of the bed, household belongings strewn everywhere.

When in 1983, I finally lost my job at the film company, I was at a terrible loss as to where to go or what to do next. Most immediately I applied for unemployment benefits, which I received, and began doing volunteer work. I also reestablished contact with the Division of Vocational Rehabilitation.

My only source of income at this time, in addition to the unemployment benefits I was receiving, was a small monthly stipend I was receiving from a family trust fund my father, tragically, still administers. He makes reference to this in his letter of October 1980. This is taxable income, which I must always make quarterly estimated payments on. Naturally, I do not receive any entitlements along with it such as food stamps or Medical Assistance as this is not a source of income which comes from the government. My father, in particular, has always insisted it is disgraceful to live on Social Security benefits, and I, sadly, have always agreed with him and the rest of my family concerning this. In fact, I applied for Social Security benefits several times anyway. Because in my heart I have never wanted these benefits, however, I didn't bother to appeal the initial denials I received from the Disability Determination Service. I knew nothing of what subsidized housing may or may not have been available at the time.

When my unemployment benefits ran out, I began supplementing my trust fund stipend with money earned from part-time temporary jobs I obtained through temporary employment agencies.

I was continuing to suffer in my relationship with my outpatient psychiatrist at Sheppard-Pratt, as well as with the unfairness of what had been done to me there as an inmate. One day, several friends of mine who knew of my troubles told me of a mental patients' self-help group which had come into existence in Baltimore called "On Our Own, Inc." I had vaguely heard of the establishment of some kind of mental patients' movement in the early

1970s but had heard nothing else about it since then. I was not aware a chapter of it had now begun in the Baltimore area.

My friends urged me to look into this group, and I decided to take their advice. I looked up On Our Own in the phone book and found that, fortunately, they were publicly listed. I called and was given directions as to how to get to their location by transit bus. I did not know the mental patients' self-help movement was part of a rampantly libertarian social movement.

Civil libertarianism is a political philosophy that cares naught about anything else except its own extremist ideology. Human life holds no value whatsoever for libertarians.

I found the small, one-room Drop-In Center located in the northeastern part of Baltimore City. When I came in that day in March of 1984, Peg McCusker, who later on became Peg Sullivan and was the founder and executive director of the group, was the person on duty that afternoon. I spent several hours talking to Peg who, like myself, had spent time in Sheppard-Pratt, though considerably less so than I had. She claimed the reason she founded On Our Own after she was released was because of the extent to which she was incensed by her treatment while there. The following day, I returned to the Drop-In Center and met Mike Finkle, Peg's assistant, for the first time. Mike was equally enlightening and appeared supportive at the time.

I became a regular member at the Drop-In Center, showing up each day it was open. Mike and Peg observed me interacting with other members of the group. They observed my natural efforts to be supportive of other members of the group and my attempts at counseling them. I had completely forgotten my family and friends of theirs had said for years I was good at working with other people. Suddenly, this message was brought home to me, as I discovered an aptitude I didn't realize I had. In July of 1984, Mike and Peg offered me a part-time job as a peer counselor and coordinator at the Drop-In Center.

Years later, while in school, I was to learn that an essential part of any prospective mental health professional's training is for a student to undergo a period of mentoring by an established professional. Mike Finkle and Peg Sullivan served as these mentors to me. It was, initially, under their tutelage that I gained the ability to understand theory, in this case the theory of mental health. At the time, I also believed I was finding Mike's knowledge of the political and legal systems, which he passed on to me, to be an excellent complement to the political nature of the education I had received at the Stockbridge School.

In September of 1984, I had finally been accepted into a training program at the Maryland Rehabilitation Center, under the auspices of the Division of Vocational Rehabilitation. M.R.C., however, was not equipped to handle people with mental disabilities rather than physical ones at the time, and I did not fare well there. In January of 1985, I was dismissed from M.R.C. once again without having any idea where to go next. I had picked up some important survival skills while there, however. Most prominently, I learned how not to obsess about matters, to relax, and to be able to take calculated risks in order to get ahead in life. This thereby enabled me to work and function independently, a skill I critically needed to learn.

With this kind of support, I was finally able to extricate myself from the torturous trap I was in at Sheppard-Pratt. I finally left there in December of 1984 and have never returned for treatment since. Nor will I ever again.

The year of 1985 turned out to be one of tremendous growth for me. I benefited from the dual supports of involvement in On Our Own, and concurrent involvement in D.V.R. Joyously, I had found my calling in life after all, and was acquiring more and more marketable skills along the way as a result. I would sometimes spend the entire night at On Our Own's Drop-In Center doing all the clerical work the Center did not have the money to pay anyone to do. I was only too happy to do this at the time.

I was eventually appointed to serve on the Board of Directors and was then chosen president of the organization.

One day I happened to discover one of the smaller newspapers in Baltimore had done a cover story article on Sheppard-Pratt. I seized this opportunity to write a blistering editorial in response in which I ripped Sheppard from high heaven to hell. I wrote this in my then-capacity as president of On Our Own. This piece remains the article I have written which has been published in the closest to verbatim form.

Several weeks later, *Newsweek* magazine did a cover story on mental illness, to which I again responded as president of the organization and to which my response was, again, published. In ensuing years, I was to be featured in articles written in the *Baltimore Sun*, the *Baltimore Jewish Times*, the *Catonsville Times* and the *Baltimore Chronicle*. I was also to have several editorials I had written myself published, though only one of these was on the subject of mental illness. This one was heavily altered by the publication before printing.

After the first year of my devotion to On Our Own, Peg Sullivan and Mike Finkle began discovering they had nothing in common with me after all, besides the fact the three of us had been hospitalized psychiatrically. In a pattern she has repeated many times, Peg eventually began fighting with me. Mike Finkle did absolutely nothing to intervene.

In July of 1986, two years after I had begun working there, I was told the funding for my paid position had run out and supposedly could not be renewed. It suddenly sank in on me that my hard work, devotion and sacrifice had meant absolutely nothing to these two after all.

Peg Sullivan is a guttersnipe woman with little formal education who, tragically, has been given a position of authority and responsibility by the rest of the mental health system in Maryland. Her complete lack of managerial skills is partially accountable for the high turnover rate of her Drop-In Center staff. Sadly, because the program she runs has fewer than 15 employees, she and Mike Finkle are able to avoid the mandate of the state law that periodically protects the right of disabled individuals to work. One would think that for an organization whose stated mission is to protect and advocate the rights of other primary consumers of mental health services (including the right to work), it would not be necessary to subject them to state law. Such is not the case, however, at On Our Own.

Mike Finkle, another Jew, is Peg's spineless stool pigeon. Mike's political opinions are very capable of changing with the wind. Anyone who can put on a good enough show can make an impression on Mr. Mike. His undying, and disgusting, love for the legal establishment in particular, is entirely a product of his very sheltered upbringing.

Neither Peg Sullivan nor Mike Finkle have spent anywhere near as much time incarcerated in mental institutions as the majority of the rest of us have. Neither has ever been homeless or in jail. As such, many of us resent the fact they have been authorized by the system (not by us) to represent our points of view. Each is paid a salary of some $26,000 per year to remain quiet. Additionally, and in response, they are afforded the opportunity to dominate the patients' rights movement in Maryland. The Maryland mental health system does not consider the funding of other self-help groups to be a priority when many of these groups would oppose what that system has historically gotten away with. As such, neither Peg Sullivan nor Mike Finkle has any sense of scruples whatsoever. In the case of Peg Sullivan, she also has no common sense.

I held several different jobs after my dismissal from On Our Own, though all of these came to an end. At length, I could not even draw unemployment benefits any longer since I was losing so many jobs in such a short period of time. Had it not been for infusions of money from Elyse, I would have been forced into homelessness once again.

Chapter Twenty-Eight

When I began seeing a psychiatrist some place other than Sheppard-Pratt, this person noticed how sedated I was on Mellaril. He immediately switched me to another similar kind of medication, but one which was less sedative. My subsequent discovery that I was now able to get out of bed in the morning was a contributing factor to my ill-fated elation back in 1985. The difficulty was that unbeknownst to any of my previous irresponsible psychiatrists, Mellaril is used in the treatment of depression as well as schizophrenia. While I was considerably less sedated on the new major tranquilizer my new psychiatrist had put me on, this drug did not have the antidepressant effect Mellaril does. Thus, by 1987, I was in the midst of a terrible, terrible depression, though no one, myself included, was aware this was what was happening to me. It would be another year and a half before anyone would put me on any anti-depressant medication, enabling me to discover I felt better on a combination of both major tranquilizer and anti-depressant.

During this period, my relationships with Sylvia and Tookie truly plummeted. Neither of them has ever had the capacity to accept the fact I have not been responsible for the major portion of the traumas that have befallen me in life. Thus, when I was suffering through the worst of my untreated depression in 1987 and 1988, they considered my behavior to have been even more asinine than that which they felt I had displayed for years anyway. Tookie refused to acknowledge my presence any longer. Both treated me with an attitude of absolute contempt.

Under these circumstances, I felt very isolated living alone. By complete coincidence, an acquaintance whom I had met through a mutual friend called me and asked if I wanted to move in with him. He explained that our mutual friend, who was his roommate, was moving out, and he needed somebody to replace him. I said yes.

I was not well, however, and after eight months of living together, my roommate decided to move out, taking the lease with him. Very unscrupulously, he had discussed my personal affairs and personal circumstances with our landlord who was someone of an equally unscrupulous nature. This person refused to give me a lease of my own, as I had asked him to do, and, instead, evicted me. Although I was suffering through a depression, I was not dangerous either to myself or to anyone else. Neither was I a threat to his property. I informed him I believed there were laws in effect which would prevent him from doing this to me, and I intended to invoke them. He simply laughed in my face. In fact, there was a Maryland Fair Housing law in effect, although the federal Fair Housing Amendments Act of that year had not as yet been enacted.

The apartment from which I was facing eviction happened to be only a few blocks from the Baltimore office of the Maryland State Office of Protection and Advocacy, a nonprofit public interest law firm. The Maryland P&A was not interested in doing anything other than systems advocacy and had become notorious for refusing to help any one particular individual who was not contacting them from an inpatient psychiatric facility somewhere. Nonetheless, I hoped they might be willing to help me. I sought only an attorney, from somewhere, who would be willing to go to court for me immediately to seek an injunction against my imminent eviction.

I spoke with the then-director of the firm who informed me, of course, there wasn't anything his agency was going to do for me and suggested I go down to the local Legal Aid Bureau instead. Regrettably, he neglected to call ahead and alert them to the fact that I was coming down and had legitimate reason to be there. I had my doubts about whether they would be willing to do anything for me either, as I had been there previously as well. I had been denied help from them, in part, on the basis of their exclusionary income restrictions, by which individuals may be deemed ineligible for their help unless they are entirely indigent. I thought I would go down anyway, since I had been referred there.

I walked into the reception area and discovered, as usual, I was the only white person there. The receptionist inquired how they could help me, though with a subtle smirk on her face. I explained my predicament to her and waited to be interviewed. After a few minutes, I was led into one of their offices where a tall, black, female attorney dictated to me, loudly, that I did not meet the necessary income guidelines to qualify for their help. I became exasperated and inquired whether one simply had to be black in order to get any help there? At that point I was asked to leave. No one there was aware that simply because someone may be white and able-bodied that this does not necessarily mean they are not in legitimate need of help.

From there, I went to the Baltimore City Community Relations Commission where, at last, I was offered some understanding. I went through the initial intake procedure and then met with a Ms. Susan Randall, who was particularly helpful. A few days later, a gentleman from this agency called me at home to find out how they could further help me.

No one had ever counseled me as to how, specifically, my eviction would have been prevented even if a court injunction had have been won in my favor. I did not want the police showing up at my door and arresting me for trespassing. I was also terribly, terribly depressed. Lastly, I had succeeded in making last-minute arrangements for an alternative place to live. And so I thanked this man for his and his agency's generosity but told him I was simply going to move anyway.

At the height of this depression, I went one night to the emergency room of one of the hospitals located in downtown Baltimore and requested voluntary admission to their inpatient psychiatric unit. In what was a complete perversion of Maryland's involuntary commitment statute, I was told I would not be admitted because I was not dangerous either to myself or anyone else. One of the intriguing aspects of this situation was that I actually had a budget private insurance plan, taken out on an individual basis, which would have paid the major portion of the cost of my short-term care. I was not a Medical Assistance recipient.

I complained of this mistreatment to our state office of protection and advocacy, but as is customarily the case with them, they were not interested in doing anything about any of this.

EX-INMATE IN EXILE

In June of 1988, I was able to obtain a Section 8 housing certificate through the generosity of the Robert Wood Johnson Foundation for Mental Health. A month later, I used this to rent another studio apartment in downtown Baltimore, though in a different location from where I had lived previously. I write now from within this same apartment.

Also in July of 1988, I was offered a part-time job at one of the psychosocial rehabilitation programs in the Baltimore metropolitan area, where I remain today. After my first year of working at this program, my hours were increased to full-time status, enabling me to surrender my subsidized housing. At the present time, I am self-sustaining and hope to be able to remain so for the rest of my life.

In August of 1988, I was temporarily suspended from On Our Own's Drop-In Center, in a further example of Mike Finkle, Peg Sullivan and their cronies' ingratitude for all I had done for them and their organization. It became obvious to me, after a while, there was going to be no help whatsoever coming to me concerning this idiotic situation from within the state of Maryland. I turned to one of the leaders of the patients' rights movement elsewhere, but this was to no avail either.

More recently, I inquired of Mike Finkle why, in all the years of my losing jobs since I had met him, he had never comprehensively explained to me there was a state law in effect which might have prevented this from happening. To some extent at the time, being reasonably assured of not losing any subsequent jobs would have softened the blow of being kicked out of the one I had had at On Our Own. But Mike replied in his best arrogant voice, "I refuse to take responsibility for never telling you about the state law that protects your right to work as a disabled person!" It is questionable whether this law would have been enforced in my behalf under any circumstances due to poor enforcement by the state agency responsible for administering it. But Mike Finkle was unaware of this. As an individual, I cannot help wondering what he is being paid a good salary for if someone else is expected to take the blame for his folly. Vocational rehabilitation and supported employment programs do not inform clients of those laws that exist to protect their rights to work due to a fiscal disincentive to do so.

In 1975 Congress passed, and President Ford signed, the "Protection and Advocacy Act." For the first time, this provided money to establish nonprofit law firms in each state where attorneys would be paid to act as legal advocates for people who were considered to be developmentally disabled in any way. A major accomplishment for the mental health community was the passage by Congress in 1986 of the "Protection and Advocacy for Mentally Ill Individuals Act." This then provided some additional federal funding for attorneys to advocate on behalf of people with mental health problems as well. The difficulty with this arrangement is that the federal mandate which accompanies the money can provide an ideal opportunity for P&A staff to not do all that needs to be done to correct the mental health system. Another problem with the P&A mandate is that it provides for the input of members of such groups as the Mental Health Association and the Alliance for the Mentally Ill. These two organizations, among others, frequently do not represent patients' points of view.

EX-INMATE IN EXILE

The mental health establishment has always insisted, conspiratorially, that under no circumstances whatsoever can anyone who has a mental health problem be counted on to seek treatment voluntarily for this disability. This then supposedly justifies treating us against our will. Furthermore, doing so is considered humanitarian and even "progressive." Tragically, court systems and state legislatures have always been lulled by a combination of the mental health profession's tremendous establishmentarian appeal and the total lack of credibility suffered by patients into granting this establishment its way. This has provided an unguarded and historical open door to the abuse of patients.

That the leaders of the patients' rights movement insist on seeing themselves as "left-wing radicals," as well, makes no sense at all. The mental health system is already liberal, oppressive and patronizing; this is precisely what is wrong with it. If we are to stand in any kind of opposition to this system, we need to see ourselves as a movement of conservatives, not anything else.

All of these goings-on, both within Maryland and without (but particularly within), can only be characterized as a form of rampant masturbation. And it is in this sense that it is a complete and utter myth that women do not ejaculate as well. In fact, it has become evident that an absolute tidal wave of cum has accrued at the meatus of the Mountain of Mental Health. It is cascading everywhere.

Chapter Twenty-Nine

Liberalism and the Democratic Party will forever patronize the mental patients' movement. To expect them to do otherwise would be to continue to be foolish. The Republican Party, by contrast, is at long last beginning to look more and more like what the Democrats once did. It would not be out of step for Republicans to endorse and support both the causes of disability rights and gay rights. Though not gay myself, I am a supporter of the gay and lesbian rights movement nonetheless. Liberalism and the Democratic Party have no monopolies on political activism, progress or suffering.

The day George Bush successfully vetoed the Civil Rights Act of 1990, I heaved six sighs of relief. Life had become completely unbearable for anyone who was white in Baltimore City, particularly in the downtown neighborhood where I live.

One and one half blocks from where I live, Baltimore's militant feminists parade up and down North Charles Street all day and all night, stormtroopers every one of them. These women will look at a man (any man) as if they would cut his balls off if they could just get their hands on him (and them). Charles Street has become reminiscent of Harvard Square in Cambridge, Massachusetts, circa 1973.

In its quest to deprive many of its own citizens of what are morally their rights, Baltimore's liberal/Jewish/feminist conspiracy has gone long unchecked. Baltimore has become an idiotically-Democratic city in an anally-Democratic state. Democracy does not reign here. Totalitarianism does.

In the fall of 1987, I became a part-time undergraduate major in Mental Health and Human Services at Morgan State University here in Baltimore. I hope, ultimately, to earn a Master of Arts in Sociology.

For some ten years now, Billy's most favored expressive mantra, delivered in response to almost any comment I make, has been, "Yeah, Philip, we don't care!" They both have developed an unscrupulous way of laughing at almost any matter I happen to bring up for discussion. Perhaps this is due to chaos in their lives.

Today, Susie remains at Queens College, where she teaches American Literature. She recently obtained full professorship there. Billy continues to teach at Stonybrook University, where he is associate professor of English and Creative Writing. Both have written and published numerous books. In 1982, Susie gave birth to a gorgeous and funny little girl, a niece for Gerson and me, and a daughter for themselves. At this writing, Susie and Billy are preparing to relocate in order to assume new teaching positions at Pennsylvania State University.

The former Stockbridge School was sold in the 1970s and is now known as the Michael Desisto School. In the fall of 1988, known alumni of the old Stockbridge School received notices that Hans Maeder had passed away in September of that year, at age 78.

Elyse remains in Scarsdale, New York. She is busy caring for her grandchildren in New York and Baltimore and doing anything else she can possibly do to be helpful to her children. We remain in contact by phone and by mail, and I rarely visit New York without visiting her, something I'm welcome to do. In the years between my mother's passing in 1968 and 1989, Elyse never once refused a collect telephone call from me, no matter from what far-flung corner of the earth I was calling. I no longer call collect.

My father, who is now 84 years old, lives in retirement in California. Once each year, he comes to Baltimore to see Gerson and me, family friends, and sometimes Sylvia and Tookie. After spending three or four days here, he heads up to New York to visit Susie, Billy, and his granddaughter for several more days. He then goes to Massachusetts to visit his relatives there before heading back to the West Coast. Gerson frequently travels across country to visit him, as well.

Sylvia and Tookie live in comfortable retirement here in Baltimore, though in recent years they have suffered health problems. Many of their former friends have passed away, but they remain as active as possible in social and cultural events. We remain in contact by phone.

My mother's sister, Helen Gene, passed away in Florida in May of 1989. Her husband, my uncle Leonard who was always a favorite of our family, passed away in August of 1990.